How to Beat Your Dad at Chess

Murray Chandler

Lister

HOW TO
BEAT YOUR
DAD AT
CHESS

First published in the UK by Gambit Publications Ltd 1998.
Reprinted 2000, 2001, 2002 (twice), 2003, 2004, 2005, 2006, 2007, 2009, 2010, 2011

ISBN-13: 978-1-901983-05-0
ISBN-10: 1-901983-05-6

DISTRIBUTION:
Worldwide (except USA): Central Books Ltd, 99 Wallis Rd, London E9 5LN, England.
Tel +44 (0)20 8986 4854 Fax +44 (0)20 8533 5821. E-mail: orders@Centralbooks.com

Gambit Publications Ltd, 99 Wallis Rd, London E9 5LN, England.
E-mail: info@gambitbooks.com
Website (regularly updated): www.gambitbooks.com

Edited by Graham Burgess
Typeset by John Nunn
Printed in Great Britain by the MPG Books Group, Bodmin and King's Lynn.

*This book is dedicated to Graham Chandler (my Dad of course!),
and also to my brother Keith, who checked all the positions.*

Gambit Publications Ltd
Managing Director: GM Murray Chandler
Chess Director: GM John Nunn
Editorial Director: FM Graham Burgess
German Editor: WFM Petra Nunn
Webmaster: Dr Helen Milligan WFM

Acknowledgements: David Stanley (cover), Harvey Lister (drawings), Tim Wall,
Sheila Jackson, Ken Whyld, Alex Meynell, Keith Chandler, Paul Harrington.

Contents

The 50 Deadly Checkmating Patterns

Introduction

This book is for every chess-player who regularly faces – and loses – to opponents stronger than themselves. This could be at work, down the chess club, at school, in tournaments, or, as for many youngsters, at home, playing Dad. In fact for 'Dad' read anyone who constantly outplays you, grinds you down, takes your pieces and checkmates you.

Each of the '50 Deadly Checkmates'[1] catalogued here explains a specific *theme* used to attack the opponent's king. These themes are recurring, and crop up again and again in chess games – virtually regardless of the level of the players, or the precise placement of the pieces. Top chess players are very skilled at recognizing these basic patterns. By learning the key elements it becomes much easier and quicker to find winning combinations.

One qualifying criterion for the 50 Deadly Checkmates was that each theme should arise at least fairly frequently in actual practice. Some of the themes occur all the time. Whatever your level of play, there will be many opportunities to employ these attacking concepts.

So, if you really want revenge over Dad – here it is!

Murray Chandler

---

1 To be completely accurate, there are 47 *checkmating* strategies. Number 11 shows how to save a difficult game with perpetual check, and Numbers 10 and 12 are themes to win material.

Only a fraction of these attacking themes had existing names (even though chess history dates back several hundred years). To describe previously uncategorized themes, poetic licence has been used where a famous game illustrates the concept. These are *The Petrosian Draw* (Checkmate 11) *Taimanov's Knight Check* (Checkmate 9), *The Korchnoi Manoeuvre* (Checkmate 28), *Blackburne's Other Mate* (Checkmate 38), and *The Fischer Trap* (Checkmate 50).

Algebraic Notation

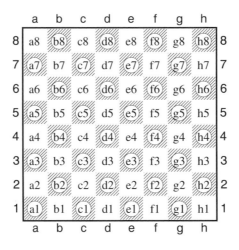

The chess notation used in this book is the simple, algebraic notation in use throughout the world. It can be learnt by anyone in just a few minutes.

As you can see from the chessboard above, the files are labelled a-h (going from left to right) and the ranks are labelled 1-8. This gives each square its own unique reference point. The pieces are described as follows:

Knight   =   ♞
Bishop   =   ♝
Rook   =   ♜
Queen   =   ♛
King   =   ♚

Pawns are not given a symbol. When they move simply the *destination square* is given.

The following additional symbols are also used:

Check   =   +
Double Check   =   ++
Capture   =   x
Castles kingside   =   0-0
Castles queenside   =   0-0-0
Good move   =   !
Bad move   =   ?

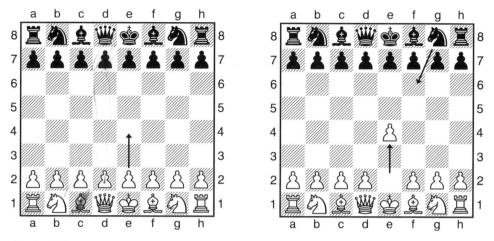

In the left-hand diagram above White is about to play the move **1 e4**. The **1** indicates the move number, and **e4** the destination square of the white pawn.

In the right-hand diagram White's **1 e4** move is complete. Black is about to reply **1...♘f6** (moving his knight to the **f6-square** on his *first move*).

7

How Chess Masters Think

If you were to visit a chess tournament and watch a grandmaster in action, you would be able to observe a surprising range of emotions. Sometimes, in apparently simple positions, the grandmaster might lapse into lengthy periods of concentration, where ten minutes or more might be spent on a move. At other times the moves will come very quickly, even in complicated positions. You might even be shocked if the grandmaster suddenly wins the game with a lengthy and brilliant mating sacrifice – after thinking for just a few seconds. Clearly the analytical process is not always directly related to how complicated the position is on the surface.

The reason for this is pattern recognition. If the grandmaster can recall similar positions encountered in the past, the same themes and concepts *might* be applicable to the game in hand. This makes it much easier and quicker to analyse a position. It especially applies to the most basic attacking formations around the enemy king. Once a known motif is spotted, the moves of the potential combination are analysed to check that it does indeed work in the particular position on the board.

It is clear then that chess analysis is a mixture of *calculation of individual moves* and *pattern recognition.*

Effectively *all* chessplayers think in this way (consciously or otherwise!). However, the ratio between these two methods of thought is different for players of varying strengths. Although no scientific tests have been done, inexperienced players use perhaps 95% calculation and 5% pattern recognition. For master-strength players the figure is more like 40% calculation and 60% pattern recognition. Logically, therefore, learning to recognize more key patterns could help dramatically improve your chess strength.

In this book we will shortly cover the 50 most deadly checkmating patterns, all of which involve direct attacks on the enemy king. But first of all, a little illustration of how we recognize and remember chess 'patterns'.

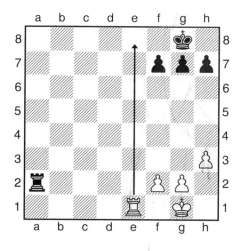

1) White moves

In the simple position above White plays 1 ♖e8 checkmate, as indicated by the arrow. If you tried, could you remember this position tomorrow? Quite likely. Even if you could not recall exactly where each white pawn was, you would almost certainly remember the essence of the combination – White giving a checkmate on the back rank with his rook.

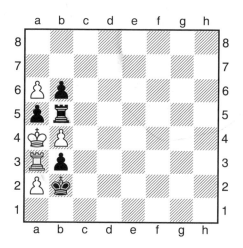

2) White moves

This position is very artificial and would never occur in a real game. Although it contains the same quantity of pieces and pawns as the previous diagram, it is hard for a chess-player to memorize this illogical position. Unlike diagram 1, there are *no familiar patterns* to assist, and each piece must be remembered individually.

If asked, some strong chessplayers would be able to recall the logical position number 1 perfectly, weeks or even months after being shown it. However, the bizarre nature of position number 2 would make the same task very difficult, and even a master might struggle to recollect it a day later. Over the years a number of psychological experiments have been conducted, using players of varying abilities, which have reaffirmed this point. The results have proved strong chess players are not very much better than ordinary players at recalling totally random positions. However, where it comes to reconstructing positions from actual games, the strong chess players are sensational. Their ability to remember *patterns* – familiar formations or clusters of pieces and pawns – is exceptionally highly developed.

Anatomy of a Combination

A big advantage of knowing the most common middlegame mating themes is that it makes the calculation of the variations so much easier. The combination below was found in a rapidplay game by a strong club player. It is very long, and can be seen illustrated with more diagrams in Deadly Checkmate 8.

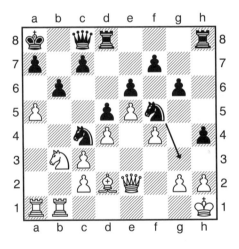

3) Black moves

In the above diagram the win goes 1...♘g3+ 2 hxg3 hxg3+ 3 ♔g1 ♖h1+ 4 ♔xh1 ♖h8+ 5 ♔g1 ♖h1+ 6 ♔xh1 ♕h8+ 7 ♔g1 ♕h2+ 8 ♔f1 ♕h1 checkmate.

An eight-move combination, sacrificing a knight and two rooks to force mate. Fantastic! Yet when shown the position, the famous Grandmaster John Nunn found the combination *in just two seconds*. Interestingly the PC Program Fritz 5, running on a Pentium, took several minutes to find the forced win. It is remarkable that a human brain is able to solve a purely tactical position faster than a powerful computer. The reason lies in the thought-processes that the experienced human players are using. First some very similar attacking patterns are recalled, which substantially reduces the amount of calculation needed. In the above example, because the combination is so long, the human player may be mentally combining *several* basic themes recalled from past experience. In this case we can guess fairly accurately at four constituent parts of the combination:

Mating with the Queen on h2/h1	**The Rook Decoy Sacrifice**
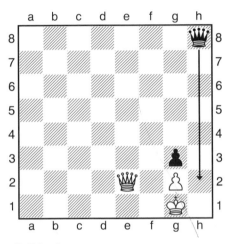	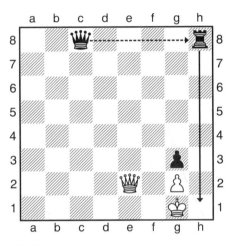

4) Black moves

Stripped of irrelevant pieces, diagram 4 shows the key position reached after Black's sixth move in the combination. 1...♛h2+ 2 ♔f1 ♛h1 is mate.

5) Black moves

This attacking pattern is also familiar. In diagram 5, the decoy sacrifice 1...♜h1+ 2 ♔xh1 ♛h8+ enables Black to bring his queen into the attack with gain of tempo.

The Taimanov Knight Check	The Knight Fork

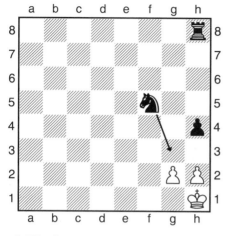

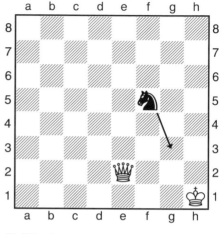

6) Black moves

In diagram 6, 1...♘g3+ 2 hxg3 hxg3+ is a common theme for forcing open the h-file to get at White's king.

7) Black moves

1...♘g3+ forks the white king and queen. This basic tactic is relevant to the combination of diagram 3, as it *forces* White to capture Black's knight.

As you can see, diagrams 4-7 contain the 'building blocks' that led to the combination in diagram 3. The strong club player showed praiseworthy ability in recalling these themes, and correctly deciding (by exact calculation) whether the combination was possible *in this unique position*. Grandmaster Nunn, with his vast experience, took a mental short-cut. As well as recognizing Damiano's Mate (from Checkmate 8), he recalled the whole exact pattern from games he had encountered in the past.

Remembering the Basic Attacking Patterns is Easy

Learning the basic theme behind each of the 50 Deadly Checkmates will improve your game both quickly and permanently:

a) Almost *any* kingside attack you play will involve elements of one of the Deadly Checkmates. While you will still have to use all of your skills and abilities to calculate combinations, it will be much easier to find them.

b) Themes and patterns are much easier to remember than opening traps or opening moves. Once imprinted on the memory they tend to stay with you for life.

c) You will enjoy your chess games much more. Instead of groping in the dark for a plan, manoeuvre your pieces towards Dad's king – and attack!

What do I do if Dad won't castle?

The majority of the 50 themes in this book deal with attacks against a king that has castled on the kingside. This is because the kingside is by far the most common place for the defending king to end up. Not only is the king safest in the corner, but castling is very important to complete the development of the pieces.

If your opponent refuses to castle early, but you can't see a strong continuation to exploit his king position in the centre, don't worry. Just develop your pieces on active squares, and centralize your rooks, and you will soon very likely have a big advantage in position.

When Black is White and vice versa...

Every position in this book (excluding a handful of basic examples) *is based on an actual game*. This gives a sense of drama and realism, compared to 'pure' positions especially composed to illustrate a theme. In real life pieces and pawns often lurk in inconvenient places, and you have to learn to take them into account with each combination.

In the same spirit, many positions feature *Black* to move (in some chess books all of the examples are exclusively with White to play). However, for practical purposes, the text introducing each Deadly Checkmate always refers to the position from *White's* point of view. If a white rook sacrifice on g7 is advocated, it automatically follows that if Black is the aggressor he could make the same rook sacrifice on the g2-square.

Finally, a small number of the basic positions show just part of a chessboard (for space reasons) or are missing a white or black king (where the piece is irrelevant to the theme). Obviously this is for illustrative purposes only. It will not occur in a real game, unless for some strange reason Dad breaks your chessboard in half and hides the pieces.

DEADLY CHECKMATE 1	**Anastasia's Mate**

Your secret weapon: a knight on e7

Even strong players can fall for this one! The name Anastasia's Mate is derived from a novel, *Anastasia und das Schachspiel* by Wilhelm Heinse, published in 1903, which has an example in the book.

The key components of this neat little trap are:

a) *a white knight on the e7-square;*

b) *a black pawn on g7; and*

c) *a black king on the h8-square.*

This formation has a particular hidden danger for the defender. The white knight on e7 takes away two key potential flight squares from the black king – the g8-square and the g6-square. Therefore if White can some arrange to check on the h-file with a queen or rook, and Black has no piece to interpose, the result is mate. *This justifies White sacrificing heavily (for example, on the h7-square) to force open the h-file.*

Typical Pattern for Anastasia's Mate

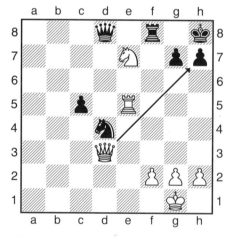

8a) White moves

The white rook is poised to transfer to the h-file, which White forces open with the queen sacrifice 1 ♕xh7+. Black must capture with 1...♔xh7 *(8b)*.

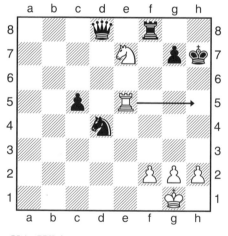

8b) White moves

The rook swings across to h5 giving checkmate. The black king has no escape, as the white knight on e7 controls the flight squares g8 and g6.

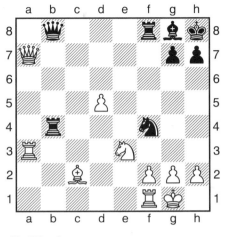

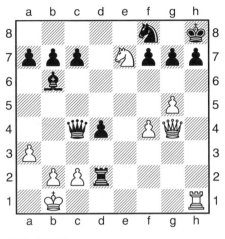

9) Black moves

The white position looks solid, but appearances prove deceptive, as Black can checkmate in just three moves: 1...♘e2+ 2 ♔h1 ♕xh2+! 3 ♔xh2 ♖h4.

10) White moves

1 ♖xh7+! and now 1...♘xh7 2 ♕c8+ ♘f8 3 ♕xf8+ ♔h7 4 ♕g8 is mate. That leaves 1...♔xh7, when White can choose between 2 ♕h5, 2 ♕h4 and 2 ♕h3 – all mate!

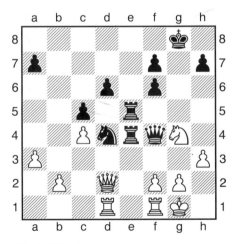

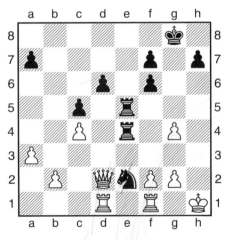

11a) Black moves

As mate is the final result, spectacular sacrifices to open the h-file are possible. First Black sacrifices the queen with 1...♘e2+ 2 ♔h1 ♕xg4! 3 hxg4 (*11b*).

11b) Black moves

How does Black check on the h-file with White's pawn on g4 in the way? The solution is a stunning rook sacrifice: 3...♖h5+! 4 gxh5 ♖h4 checkmate.

The Missing Defensive f-pawn

An absent f-pawn makes the diagonal longer

The black f7-pawn is important for defence. If it has been moved, lost or exchanged, the castled king is often more vulnerable.

This is particularly the case when White has a bishop placed on the a2-g8 diagonal (usually on the c4- or b3-square). Black's king is usually on the h8-square, shielded from attack by its own pawns on g7 and h7. The problem is that *the black king has very few escape squares, as the white bishop controls the g8-square*.

If White can administer a check with queen or rook on the h-file, the black king is invariably in major trouble. White's goal is therefore to open the h-file in any way possible, which usually means a sacrifice.

Typical Pattern with the Missing f7-pawn

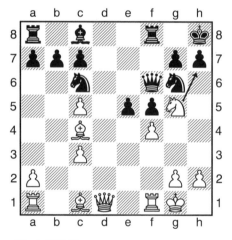

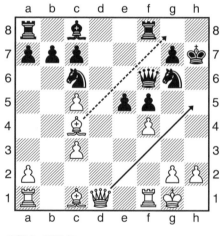

12a) White moves

The black king is currently shielded by the h7-pawn. White sacrifices his knight with 1 ♘xh7 ♔xh7 *(12b)*, opening the h-file.

12b) White moves

There follows 2 ♕h5 checkmate. Note how the white bishop on c4 prevents the black king escaping (via g8) *because there is no black pawn on f7*.

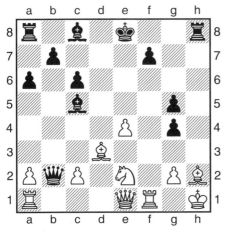

13) Black moves

Here the h-file is already open, and the black rook is itching to exploit this. After 1...罩xh2+ 2 當xh2 豐h8+ White is mated following 3 當g3 豐h4.

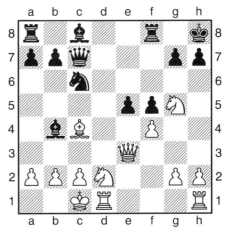

14) White moves

After 1 ♘xh7 當xh7 2 豐h3+ 當g6 White has to close in with the queen: 3 豐g3+ 當h7 (3...當f6 4 豐g5 is mate) 4 豐h4+ 當g6 5 豐g5+ 當h7 6 豐h5 mate.

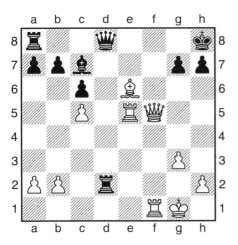

15a) White moves

Before sacrificing the queen, it must be established that the black king cannot escape to safety via the g6-square. White plays 1 豐xh7+ 當xh7 2 罩h5+ *(15b)*.

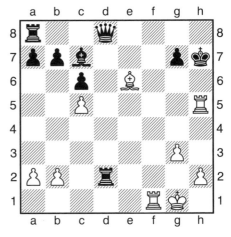

15b) Black moves

The king can escape – but only temporarily. After 2...當g6 comes the pretty finish 3 皇f7 checkmate.

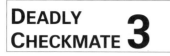

DEADLY CHECKMATE **3** | The Arabian Mate

Rook & knight have got real bite

In the late middlegame and endgame, rooks come into their own. Rooks are at their most effective on open files and ranks, which is usually in the later stages of the game (by which time various pieces and pawns have been exchanged off). If a rook is able to penetrate to the opposing seventh or eighth rank, it often puts the opponent under pressure. Add in *a white knight on the f6-square*, and a very common kind of *mating-net* emerges.

This mate delivered with rook and knight is considered the earliest on record, according to Renaud and Kahn in *The Art of Checkmate*. This is because reforms were made to the powers of most of the other chess pieces in the fifteenth century. Only the rook, knight and king have always moved in the same way as they do today.

Basic Pattern for the Arabian Mate

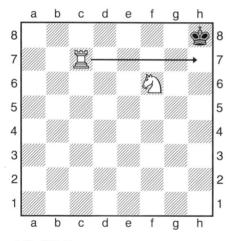

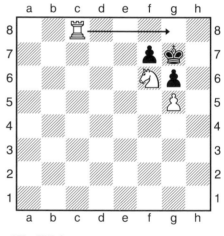

16) White moves

With the rook on the *seventh* rank, White mates with 1 ♖h7. The superbly-placed knight on f6 protects the rook and takes away g8 as a flight square.

17) White moves

With the rook on the *eighth* rank, White mates with 1 ♖g8. White's knight is protected from capture by the pawn on g5, which also covers the h6-square.

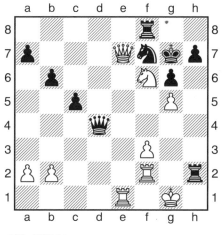

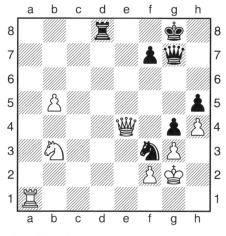

18) White moves

Although Black has some unpleasant threats, White can force mate with checks: 1 ♕xf8+ ♔xf8 2 ♖e8+ ♔g7 3 ♖g8 mate.

19) Black moves

1...♕xa1! eliminates the defender of the back rank. After 2 ♘xa1 ♖d1 White loses due to the threat of 3...♖g1 mate (as 3 ♕e8+ ♔g7 changes nothing).

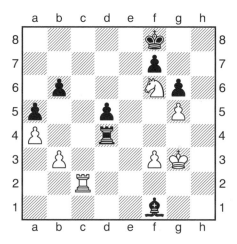

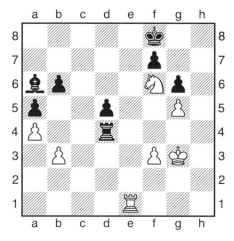

20a) White moves

The subtle 1 ♖c1! poses Black a problem (since 1...♗e2 2 ♖c8+ ♔e7 3 ♖e8+ skewers king and bishop). After the best defence, 1...♗a6, comes 2 ♖e1 (20b).

20b) Black moves

The endgame mating-net has been delicately woven by White. Black has no viable defence to the threat of 3 ♖e8+ ♔g7 4 ♖g8 checkmate.

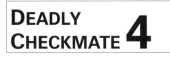

DEADLY CHECKMATE 4

Philidor's Legacy

A smothered mate your Dad will hate

This striking classic has captivated generations. The best-known version is named after François-André Philidor, a famous French player from the eighteenth century.

A smothered mate occurs when the defender's own pieces hem in his king completely – so that a check from an enemy knight delivers mate. Philidor's classic version (actually first published by Lucena in 1497) involves a beautiful queen sacrifice and then checkmate with the knight. It is perhaps the most famous middlegame theme in chess. Unfortunately, this may mean that many opponents will know and avoid it. Even so, the theme will often influence the course of a game, even if it does not actually occur on the board.

Basic Pattern for Philidor's Legacy

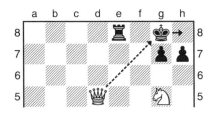

21a) Black moves

The white queen has just moved to d5, giving check. After 1...♔h8 (1...♔f8 2 ♕f7 is checkmate) White continues 2 ♘f7+ ♔g8 3 ♘h6++ *(21b)*.

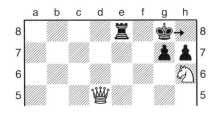

21b) Black moves

As Black is in *double check* (from the white queen *and* the white knight) the king must return with 3...♔h8 *(21c)* (as 3...♔f8 would again allow 4 ♕f7 mate).

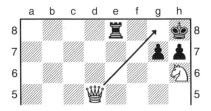

21c) White moves

Now comes the sparkling queen sacrifice, as given in virtually all training manuals: 4 ♕g8+ ♖xg8 *(21d)*.

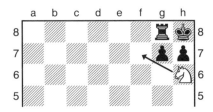

21d) White moves

Black's rook has been forced to block in his own king. The white knight triumphantly returns with 5 ♘f7 checkmate.

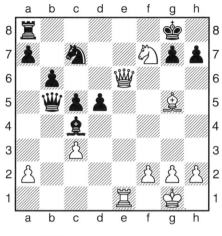

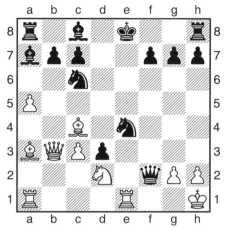

22) White moves

The attack on the queen by Black's knight is irrelevant because White's first move gives *double check*. 1 ♘h6++ ♔h8 2 ♕g8+ ♖xg8 3 ♘f7 checkmate.

23) Black moves

It looks like Black is in trouble, but a stunning *decoy sacrifice* unpins the black knight and turns the tables. 1...♕g1+ 2 ♖xg1 ♘f2 mate.

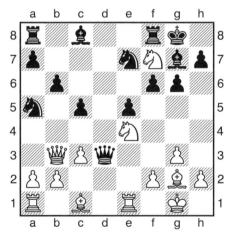

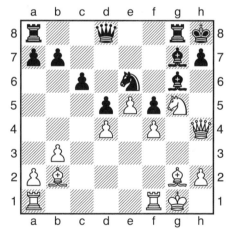

24) White moves

If Black can keep the f7-square covered, a draw by perpetual check is likely with 1 ♘h6++ ♔h8 2 ♘f7+, etc. Here 2 ♕g8+?? is a blunder due to 2...♘xg8! 3 ♘f7+ ♖xf7.

25) White moves

Only the black bishop on g6 is preventing immediate smothered mate by the knight. White wins with the decoy sacrifice 1 ♕xh7+ ♗xh7 2 ♘f7 mate.

21

DEADLY CHECKMATE 5

Semi-Smothered Mate

The forgotten mate

Because the 'Philidor's Legacy' mate (Deadly Checkmate 4) is so well known, some related formations have been rather overlooked.

In a semi-smothered mate the defending king is only partially hemmed in by its own pieces. The most common form (as in the normal Smothered Mate) features a preliminary thunderbolt of a queen sacrifice to eliminate a flight square. This is followed by checkmate with the knight.

These semi-smothered hybrids are rarer and less well known than the normal smothered mates, and even master-strength players have been trapped by them.

Typical Pattern for Semi-Smothered Mate

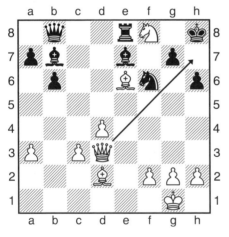

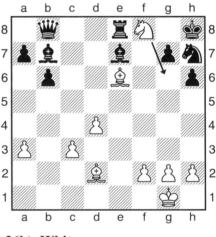

26a) White moves

The white queen is sacrificed with 1 ♕h7+. Black is forced to reply 1...♘xh7 *(26b)* (as White's knight on f8 covers the queen and prevents ...♔xh7).

26b) White moves

Now that Black has had to self-block his own h7-square, White plays 2 ♘g6 checkmate. Note how the white bishop on e6 controls the g8-square.

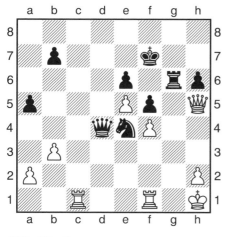

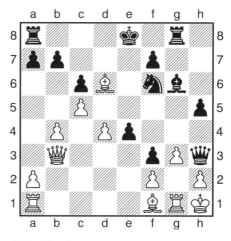

27) Black moves

If 1...♘f2+ White escapes with 2 ♖xf2, but does Black have anything better? In fact the startling 1...♕g1+ 2 ♖xg1 ♘f2 is a typical semi-smothered mate.

28) Black moves

The white bishop has just moved to f1, in order to eject the black queen from h3. Instead of retreating, Black plays 1...♘g4 2 ♗xh3 ♘xf2 checkmate.

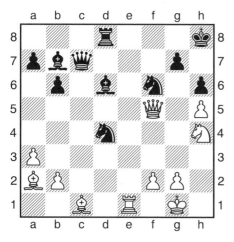

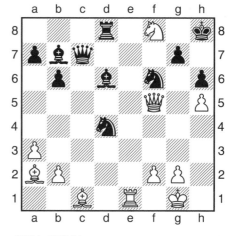

29a) White moves

After 1 ♘g6+ Black must allow the double check 1...♔h7 2 ♘f8++, but assumes that after 2...♔h8 (*29b*) White will repeat moves with another knight check.

29b) White moves

However, the white bishop raking the a2-g8 diagonal signals the possibility of semi-smothered mate. White forces mate: 3 ♕h7+ ♘xh7 4 ♘g6.

23

Single Rook Sacrifice on h8

Impress your friends with this nifty decoy sacrifice

This concept is simple and yet dramatic: White's rook is sacrificed on the empty h8-square. The idea is that when Black captures, the white queen can enter the attack, either coming to the h-file with gain of time, or mating immediately on h7.

The single rook sacrifice on h8 is always either (or both):

1) a *decoy sacrifice*, where the black king is lured onto a square it most definitely does not want to be on;

2) a *vacating sacrifice*, where the white rook is sacrificed to clear a square for the white queen.

These are bread-and-butter tactical themes for the bold attacking player.

Typical Pattern for the Single Rook Sacrifice on h8

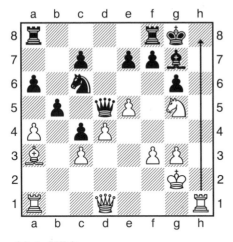

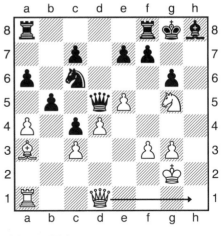

30a) White moves

After 1 ♖h8+! Black can accept the rook sacrifice in two ways. 1...♔xh8 2 ♕h1+ ♔g8 3 ♕h7 is mate, so Black captures with 1...♗xh8 *(30b)*.

30b) White moves

With 2 ♕h1 the white queen moves to the square vacated by the rook last move. Black cannot prevent mate, e.g. 2...♖fc8 3 ♕h7+ ♔f8 4 ♕xh8.

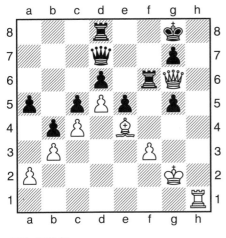

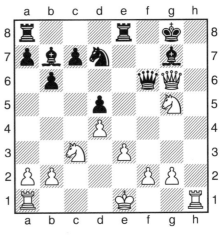

31) White moves

If 1 ♕h7+ the black king can safely move to f8 or f7, so White inserts the killer decoy sacrifice 1 ♖h8+. After 1...♔xh8 comes 2 ♕h7 checkmate.

32) White moves

Here White is a piece down. However, he swoops in to turn the tables with exactly the same rook decoy idea: 1 ♖h8+ ♔xh8 2 ♕h7 mate.

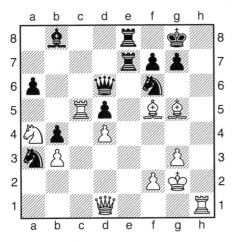

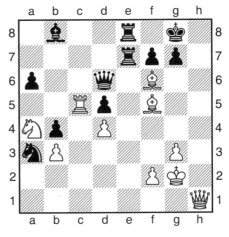

33a) White moves

In this extended version the move-order is important. After 1 ♖h8+! ♔xh8 2 ♕h1+ ♔g8 White now liquidates an important defender with 3 ♗xf6 (33b).

33b) Black moves

Black is lost whatever he plays! White's threat is 4 ♕h7+ ♔f8 5 ♕h8 checkmate, and 3...g6 fails to 4 ♕h8 checkmate. A delightful concept.

Double Rook Sacrifice on h8

'Double, double, toil and trouble; now his h-file's vulnerubble'

If the h-file is open (i.e. cleared of pawns) conditions are perfect for a direct attack with the heavy artillery of the chessboard – the queen and rooks. In such circumstances always consider if it is possible either to *double your rooks* or to *double up with queen and rook*. If so, the h-file is transformed into a virtual freeway leading directly to your opponent's king.

Once in place, the heavy pieces represent a mighty attacking force. Depending on which kingside formation Black has adopted, there remains the question of how to smash down the defensive fortress. This can require real determination when Black has a fianchettoed bishop on g7 (one of the most solid defensive structures), and the various methods are well worth learning.

Typical Pattern for the Double Rook Sacrifice on h8

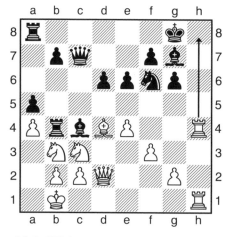

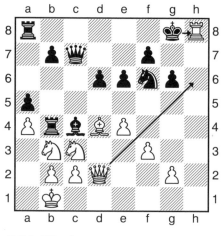

34a) White moves

The rooks are nicely doubled on the h-file – but Black's bishop on g7 stops the white queen joining the attack. There follows 1 ♖h8+ ♗xh8 2 ♖xh8+ *(34b)*.

34b) Black moves

At the cost of two rooks the black bishop has been eliminated. 2...♔xh8 3 ♕h6+ ♔g8 4 ♗xf6 leaves Black facing unstoppable mate by ♕h8.

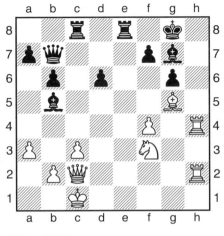

35a) White moves

The stunning 1 ♖h8+! is again aimed at eliminating the g7-bishop. Then 1...♗xh8 2 ♖xh8+ ♔g7! *(35b)* is the best try (as 2...♔xh8 loses to 3 ♗f6+ ♔g8 4 ♕h2).

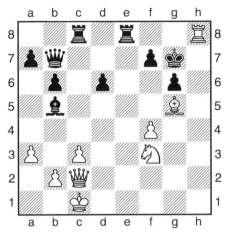

35b) White moves

The combination continues with a further rook decoy sacrifice: 3 ♖h7+! ♔xh7 (3...♔f8 4 ♗f6) 4 ♕h2+ ♔g7 (4...♔g8 5 ♗f6) 5 ♕h6+ ♔g8 6 ♗f6 forces mate.

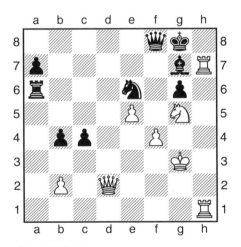

36a) White moves

Once again, both white rooks are sacrificed for a single tempo. With 1 ♖h8+ ♗xh8 2 ♖xh8+ ♔xh8 *(36b)*. Black's king is decoyed onto the h-file.

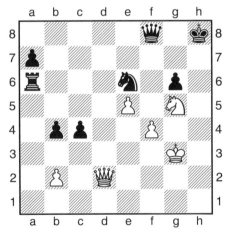

36b) White moves

Now comes yet another forcing move: 3 ♕h2+ *(with check)*, and Black still has no time to defend. 3...♔g8 and 3...♔g7 are both met by 4 ♕h7 checkmate.

<table>
<tr><td>**DEADLY**</td><td rowspan="2">**8**</td><td rowspan="2">**Damiano's Mate**</td></tr>
<tr><td>**CHECKMATE**</td></tr>
</table>

DEADLY CHECKMATE 8 — Damiano's Mate

A mate even older than Dad

Pedro Damiano published this spectacular checkmate in 1512, nearly 500 years ago.

The circumstances for this checkmate do not arise very often, but every master player can spot the idea in seconds. Both white rooks are sacrificed on the empty square h8, in a forcing five-move combination where every white move administers a check. The purpose of the rook sacrifices is threefold. A line is opened for the white queen along the first rank, a square is cleared (for the queen) on h1, and the black king is decoyed to the h-file.

Typical Pattern for Damiano's Mate

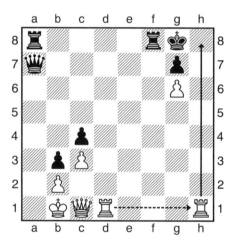

37a) White moves

As Black has winning threats of his own, every white move must come with check. White plays 1 Rh8+ Kxh8 2 Rh1+ Kg8 3 Rh8+ Kxh8 (*37b*).

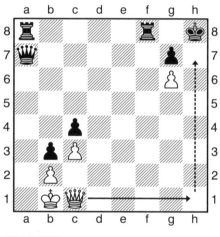

37b) White moves

Now that both white rooks are gone, the queen has access to the h1-square. There follows 4 Qh1+ Kg8 5 Qh7 checkmate.

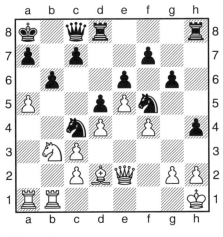

38a) Black moves

Once you recognize the patterns, even very lengthy combinations can be found quickly. Black begins with a knight sacrifice: 1...♘g3+ 2 hxg3 hxg3+ 3 ♔g1 *(38b)*.

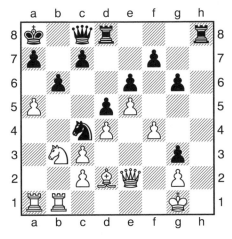

38b) Black moves

The familiar features of Damiano's Mate now suddenly appear. 3...♖h1+! 4 ♔xh1 ♖h8+ 5 ♔g1 ♖h1+ 6 ♔xh1 *(38c)*.

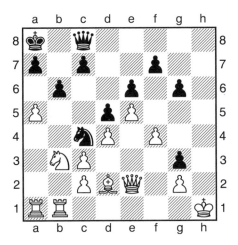

38c) Black moves

After sacrificing the two rooks on the h1-square, Black's queen comes to the h-file *with check*: 6...♕h8+ 7 ♔g1 ♕h2+ 8 ♔f1 *(38d)*.

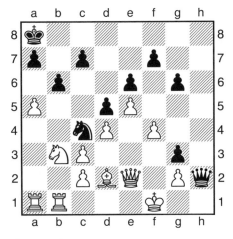

38d) Black moves

And finally, 8...♕h1 checkmate. Because it is comprised of several common patterns, this nine-move long combination is relatively simple!

Taimanov's Knight Check

A knight to remember

Opening the h-file by sacrificing a piece for the enemy h-pawn is a familiar concept, but such blunt methods are not always available. A more subtle motif involves the sacrifice of a white knight on the g6-square, diagonally in front of the h-pawn. I have dubbed this 'Taimanov's Knight Check', after the wonderful game Karpov-Taimanov, Leningrad 1977, where the theme was used to defeat a reigning world champion. The concept does, of course, pre-date that game. A variation of the motif was published in a book in 1619!

One advanced version of this theme even makes it possible to *force open an h-file that is completely closed* (i.e. where both the white and black h-pawns are still on the board). For this particular manoeuvre the h-pawn of the attacker first needs to be advanced to the fifth rank, prior to giving the knight check.

Typical Pattern for Taimanov's Knight Check (advanced version)

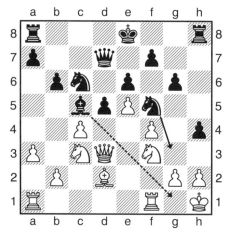

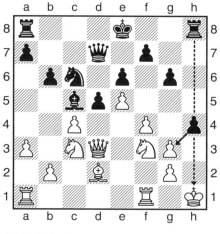

39a) Black moves

An open h-file would be disastrous for White as Black's bishop controls the g1-square. So Black plays 1...♘g3+, forcing White's capture 2 hxg3 *(39b)*.

39b) Black moves

After 2...hxg3+ the h-file is suddenly open, and White is exposed to a lethal discovered check from the black rook. 3 ♘h2 ♖xh2 is checkmate.

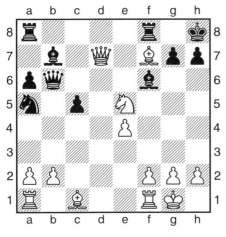

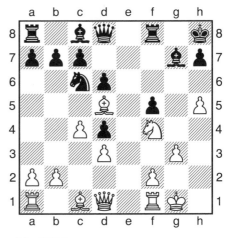

40) White moves

Control of the g8-square allows White to force open the h-file by sacrificing the knight. There follows 1 ♘g6+ hxg6 2 ♕h3+ ♗h4 3 ♕xh4 checkmate.

41) White moves

After 1 ♘g6+ hxg6 2 hxg6 Black has a free move to defend, but to no avail. He is helpless to prevent White's killer check with 3 ♕h5+ next move.

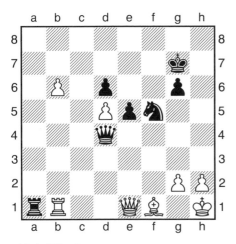

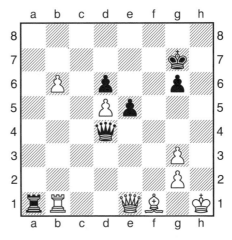

42a) Black moves

This was the magical Karpov-Taimanov game. After 1...♘g3+! White captures with 2 hxg3 (42b) (because 2 ♕xg3 allows 2...♖xb1). The h-file is now open.

42b) Black moves

There follows the brilliant rook retreat 2...♖a8!. Black wins, as White has no defence to 3...♖h8+ next move.

31

DEADLY CHECKMATE 10

The See-Saw

All you can eat on Dad's second rank

Rook checks, rook captures, rook checks, rook captures – imagine that you could make as many moves in a row as you wanted, and your opponent could only watch helplessly. Believe it or not this dream can almost come true if you set up the fearsome See-Saw. This mighty manoeuvre consists of giving alternate checks and discovered checks.

The most common See-Saw features a white rook on the g7-square, and a white bishop on the long a1-h8 diagonal. With Black's king on h8, exposed to discovered check every second move, the rook simply munches its way along the seventh rank. The hapless defender, having to move his king out of check every move, can only watch as several pieces and pawns are picked off one by one.

Basic Pattern for the See-Saw

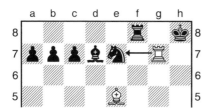

43a) White moves

After 1 ♖xe7+ Black is in a discovered check from the white bishop on e5, and must play 1...♔g8 *(43b)*.

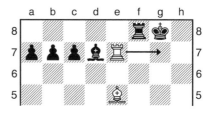

43b) White moves

With 2 ♖g7+ ♔h8, White sets up *another potential discovered check*. There follows 3 ♖xd7+ ♔g8 4 ♖g7+ ♔h8 *(43c)*.

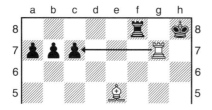

43c) White moves

The See-Saw is in full swing: 5 ♖xc7+ ♔g8 6 ♖g7+ ♔h8 7 ♖xb7+ ♔g8 8 ♖g7+ ♔h8 9 ♖xa7+ ♔g8 *(43d)*.

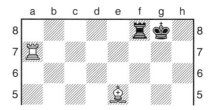

43d) White moves

A black knight, black bishop and three black pawns have been taken for nothing, and it even remains White's turn to move.

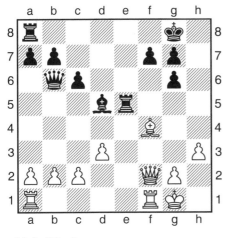

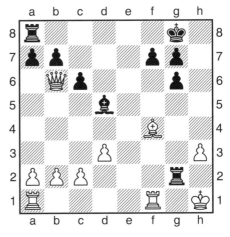

44a) Black moves

1...♖e2! exploits a *pin* on the white queen, which cannot take the rook. After 2 ♕xb6 ♖xg2+ 3 ♔h1 *(44b)* the mighty See-Saw is ready to begin.

44b) Black moves

There follows 3...♖xc2+ 4 ♔g1 ♖g2+ 5 ♔h1 ♖xb2+ 6 ♔g1 ♖g2+ 7 ♔h1 ♖xa2+ 8 ♔g1 axb6 and Black has won four pawns.

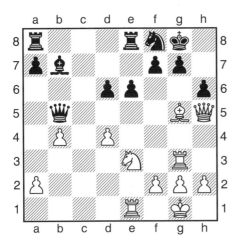

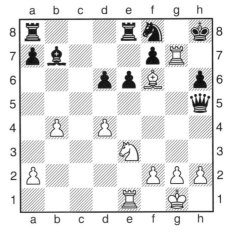

45a) White moves

Setting up a See-Saw often justifies a major investment in material. Here White sacrifices his queen with 1 ♗f6 ♕xh5 2 ♖xg7+ ♔h8 *(45b)*.

45b) White moves

After 3 ♖xf7+ ♔g8 4 ♖g7+ ♔h8 5 ♖xb7+ ♔g8 White returns for the queen: 6 ♖g7+ ♔h8 7 ♖g5+ ♔h7 8 ♖xh5 ♔g6 9 ♖h3 ♔xf6 10 ♖xh6+ and wins.

The Petrosian Draw

Not quite seventh heaven

This formation is so strong that – paradoxically – a draw is a common result. One famous example was the 12th game of the 1966 World Championship match between Tigran Petrosian and Boris Spassky in Moscow.

The position where White has a bishop occupying the long diagonal, and a rook on g7, hemming in the black king on h8, occurs in several different settings. The threat to move the rook – administering a discovered check from the bishop – is a very powerful one. So why do these types of position sometimes end in a draw?

The reason is that White has often sacrificed heavily to set up the motif. If it turns out that he will not regain sufficient material, he is usually able to force a draw by perpetual check.

Basic Patterns for the Petrosian Draw

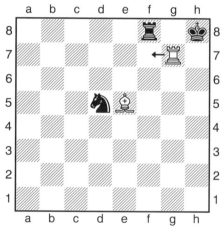

46) White moves

With this formation White can force perpetual check with 1 ♖g6+ ♔h7 2 ♖g7+, as the black h-pawn prevents Black's king escaping.

47) White moves

Here 1 ♖f7+ ♔g8 2 ♖g7+ is the correct way to force the draw, as Black's rook on f8 prevents his king escaping.

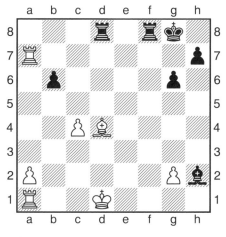

48) White moves

The pinned white bishop is saved by a perpetual check: 1 ♖g7+ ♔h8 2 ♖d7+ (the only square – 2 ♖xg6+? ♖xd4+) 2...♔g8 3 ♖g7+ with a draw.

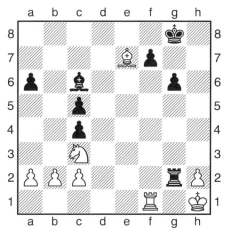

49) White moves

A piece ahead, but facing a discovered check, White forces the draw by repeatedly attacking Black's bishop: 1 ♖f6 ♗b7 2 ♖b6 ♗f3 3 ♖f6 ♗b7, etc.

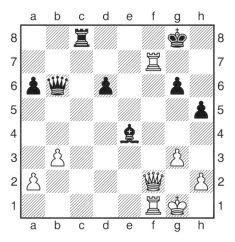

50a) Black moves

Here's a brilliant way to salvage a half point from an otherwise dead lost position: 1...♖c2! 2 ♕xb6 (2 ♖f8+ ♔g7 makes no difference) 2...♖g2+ 3 ♔h1 (50b).

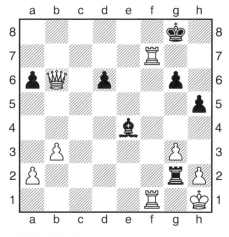

50b) Black moves

Now the black rook must choose its square precisely. 3...♖f2+! (not 3...♖xg3+ 4 ♖7f3 ♗xf3+ 5 ♖xf3) 4 ♔g1 ♖g2+ 5 ♔h1 ♖f2+! forces the draw.

The ♖h8+ & ♘xf7+ Trick

A sneaky knight fork that often wins a queen.

Watch out for this little trap when:
1) *White has a knight on g5 or e5; and*
2) *Black has castled kingside, and his h-pawn is missing.*

As the rather self-explanatory title says, the theme involves a white rook check on h8 (to decoy the black king). This is followed by the white knight capturing on f7 with check, so that the *knight forks Black's king and another piece*. Simple – and effective!

Typical Pattern for the ♖h8+ & ♘xf7+ Trick

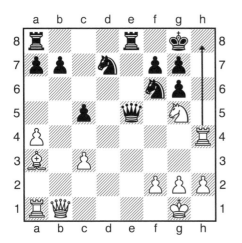

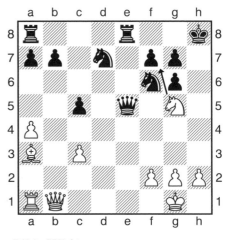

51a) White moves

A pawn ahead, Black's dreams are rudely shattered by the decoy sacrifice 1 ♖h8+. The king is forced to capture the rook with 1...♔xh8 *(51b)*.

51b) White moves

Now 2 ♘xf7+ forks the black king on h8 and the black queen on e5. As Black must move out of check, he loses his queen.

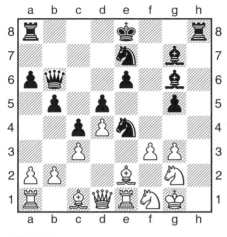

52) Black moves

The absence of a pawn on f2 makes no difference (although the idea is perhaps harder to visualize). 1...♖h1+ 2 ♔xh1 ♘f2+ forks the white king and queen.

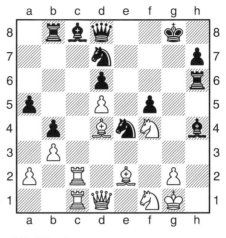

53) Black moves

This very pretty version features *two* decoy sacrifices: 1...♗f2+! 2 ♗xf2 ♖h1+ 3 ♔xh1 ♘xf2+ and again White loses the queen.

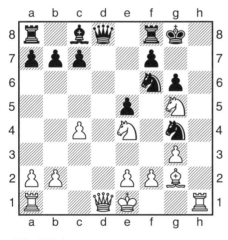

54) White moves

Even having the f7-pawn defended is no guarantee of safety. With 1 ♖h8+! ♔xh8 2 ♘xf7+ ♖xf7 3 ♕xd8+ White wins queen and pawn for rook and knight.

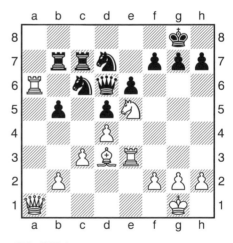

55) White moves

The h-file *can be forcibly opened* to facilitate the combination. Here 1 ♗xh7+! wins a pawn, as if 1...♔xh7, there follows 2 ♖h3+ ♔g8 3 ♖h8+ ♔xh8 4 ♘xf7+ ♔g8 5 ♘xd6.

DEADLY CHECKMATE 13

Blackburne's Mate

The kind of mate a pirate would make

Here the two bishops cooperate to deliver a mate named after the English player Joseph Blackburne (1841-1924). The title of this middlegame motif sounds a little swashbuckling, and so, indeed, is the combination. The fundamental pattern involves White having a knight on g5, and the two white bishops raking the diagonals a1-h8 and b1-h7. Usually, following a sacrifice to open lines, the black king is mated on the g8-square by the white bishop on h7.

Blackburne's Mate does not arise often, but the concept is worth knowing. Technically, there is also a rare secondary version, where White's light-squared bishop is on the a2-g8 diagonal, and Black's king is mated on h8.

Typical Pattern for Blackburne's Mate

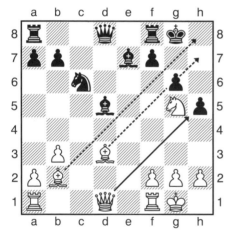

56a) White moves

Note how the white bishops (on b2 and d3) are raking the black king position. White sacrifices the queen with 1 ♕xh5 gxh5 (*56b*).

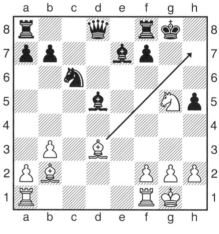

56b) White moves

Having forced opened the diagonal leading to Black's king, White plays 2 ♗h7 checkmate. The bishop is protected by the white knight on g5.

38

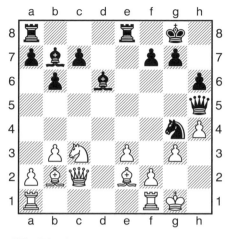

57) Black moves

1...♕xh4 wins instantly, since 2 gxh4 ♗h2 is mate. White cannot defend with 2 ♗xg4, as 2...♕h1 mate is also threatened.

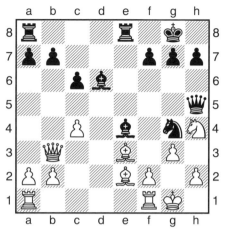

58) Black moves

After 1...♕xh4 White captures with 2 ♗xg4 (as 2 gxh4 ♗xh2 is mate). But after 2...♕xg4 Black will win easily with his extra piece.

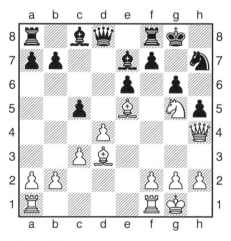

59a) White moves

Here after 1 ♕xh5 Black can try the promising-looking defence 1...♗xg5 (59b) (Black should not play 1...♘xg5 2 ♕h8 mate, nor 1...gxh5 2 ♗xh7 mate).

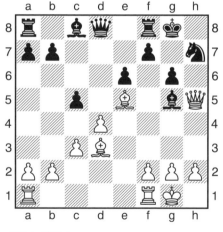

59b) White moves

However, the attacking riposte 2 ♗xg6 still wins for White. On 2...fxg6, 3 ♕xg6 is mate, and 2...♘f6 fails to 3 ♗xf6 ♕xf6 4 ♕h7 mate.

DEADLY CHECKMATE 14

Boden's Mate

If a lemming played chess, it would fall for this one

In England 1853 a friendly game Schulder-Boden ended after just 15 moves. Black's wonderful checkmate was so pretty that his name was immediately attached to the manoeuvre. The pattern arises after queenside castling, and is extremely easy for an inexperienced player to overlook. Every year there are even a few tournament-strength players who fail to recognize the danger signals and jump headlong into the trap.

The standard version involves an unexpected queen sacrifice to catch the defending king in the crossfire of two bishops.

Typical Pattern for Boden's Mate

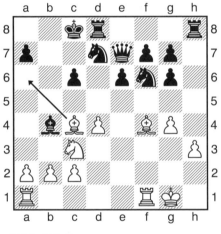

60a) White moves

Note how the bishop on f4 is controlling some important squares near the black king. The white queen is dramatically sacrificed by 1 ♕xc6+ bxc6 *(60b)*.

60b) White moves

The sacrifice has ripped open the queenside, and, remarkably, 2 ♗a6 is checkmate. Black's king is mated in the middlegame – by just two bishops!

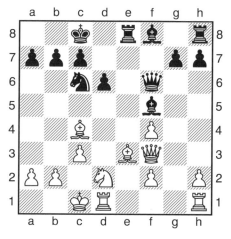

61a) Black moves

The pawn sacrifice 1...d5 frees up the black bishop on f8, and gains time by attacking the white bishop on c4. White captures with 2 ♗xd5 *(61b)*.

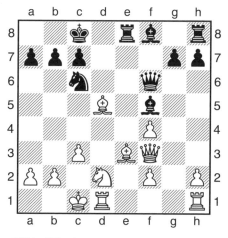

61b) Black moves

The motive behind Black's last move is revealed: 2...♕xc3+ 3 bxc3 ♗a3 mate. This is the beautiful combination played in the original Boden game.

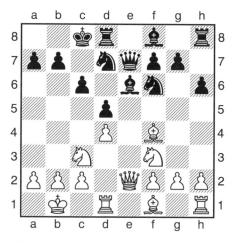

62) White moves

Here 1 ♕a6 is the spectacular winning move, as Black cannot defend the a7-pawn. If 1...bxa6, 2 ♗xa6 is mate, and 1...♘h5 loses to 2 ♕xc6+!.

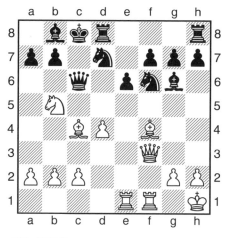

63) White moves

Here White justified an earlier piece sacrifice with the delightful winning combination 1 ♘xa7+ ♗xa7 2 ♕xc6+ bxc6 3 ♗a6 mate.

Other Queenside Mates

DEADLY CHECKMATE 15

Mate is great on b8

Queenside castling is less popular than kingside castling. One reason is that queenside castling does not automatically place the king as close to the edge of the board (where it is normally safest). This means that different attacking strategies are sometimes required. A typical combination (where Black's c-pawn has moved) involves a sacrifice on the c6-square, followed by a rook penetrating down the b-file.

For this type of tactic to end in mate, usually *the d7-square should not be available as an escape square for the black king*. Normally, in fact, d7 is blocked by one of the defender's own men. There are obvious similarities with Boden's Mate (Deadly Checkmate 14).

Typical Pattern for the Sacrifice on c6

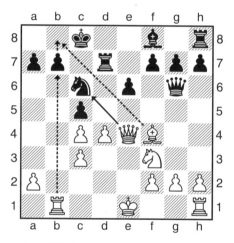

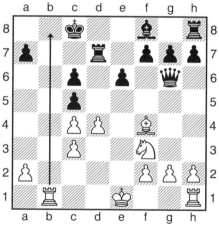

64a) White moves

The b8-square is potentially a lethal focal point, given the positions of the rook on b1 and the bishop on f4. White plays 1 ♕xc6+ bxc6 *(64b)*.

64b) White moves

The queen sacrifice has wrenched open the b-file, enabling White's rook to advance right to the eighth rank. 2 ♖b8 is checkmate.

42

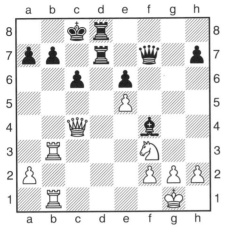

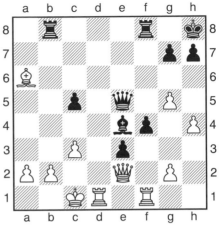

65) White moves

1 ♕xc6+ wins a pawn for nothing, as Black cannot capture the white queen. On 1...bxc6, 2 ♖b8+ ♔c7 3 ♖1b7 would be mate.

66) Black moves

A potential combination is signalled by the rook on the b-file, and the bishop on the h7-b1 diagonal. Black plays 1...♕xc3+ 2 bxc3 ♖b1 mate.

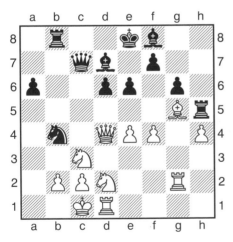

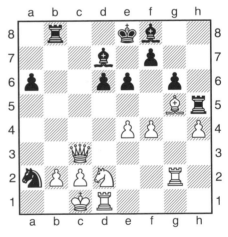

67a) Black moves

Here the clever 1...♕xc3 is easily overlooked, as White has a choice of captures. But if 2 bxc3, then 2...♘a2 mate, so White has to continue 2 ♕xc3 ♘a2+ *(67b)*.

67b) White moves

The crafty fork from the black knight does more than regain the queen. After 3 ♔b1 ♘xc3+ Black stays a piece ahead, as White's b-pawn is pinned.

DEADLY CHECKMATE **16**   The Double Rook Sacrifice

Hey Dad, take my rooks!

The term 'Double Rook Sacrifice' really refers to a specific method of giving up both rooks. Unlike most sacrifices (active moves made to expose the enemy king) here the rooks are given up in a passive manner. The opponent is allowed to capture one rook and then the other – with the rooks often being still on their original starting squares.

The aim of a Double Rook Sacrifice is to misplace the enemy queen. After capturing the second rook, the queen is usually far from the main area of activity, and unable to assist in the defence of the king. Of course, a sacrifice of either one or two rooks is a huge price to pay. The attacker needs to ensure that:

1) *the mating attack will definitely succeed after both rooks are taken; and*
2) *the opponent cannot capture just one rook and safely decline the second.*

Typical Pattern for the Double Rook Sacrifice

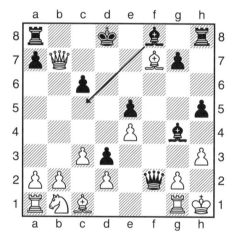

68a) Black moves

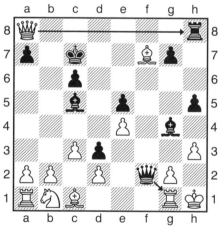

68b) White moves

As he is a piece down, Black must act incisively. Ignoring the threat to his rook on a8, he proceeds with his own attack: 1...♗c5 2 ♕xa8+ ♔c7 *(68b)*.

The white queen is now under attack from Black's other rook on h8. White can capture with 3 ♕xh8, but then comes 3...♕xg1 checkmate.

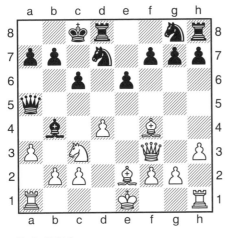

69a) White moves

An astute student might notice that Boden's Mate would be possible if Black's queen were elsewhere. White plays 1 axb4 ♛xa1+ 2 ♔d2 *(69b)*.

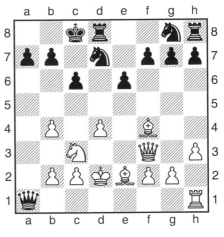

69b) Black moves

Now if 2...♛xh1 White would mate with 3 ♛xc6+ bxc6 4 ♗a6. The two white rooks have been used as bait to decoy the black queen.

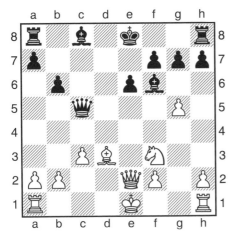

70a) Black moves

1...♗xc3+ 2 bxc3 ♛xc3+ forks king and rook, but White happily 'falls into the trap'. After 3 ♛d2 ♛xa1+ 4 ♔e2 ♛xh1 *(70b)* the black queen is out of play.

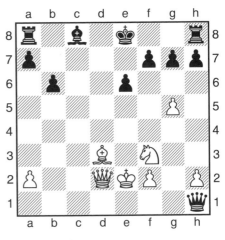

70b) White moves

A massive assault on Black's king now decides the game: 5 ♗b5+ ♗d7 (5...♔e7 6 ♛b4+ ♔d8 7 ♛d6+ ♗d7 8 ♛xd7 mate) 6 ♛xd7+ ♔f8 7 g6! hxg6 8 ♘g5 and mate with ♛xf7 follows.

45

The Double Bishop Sacrifice

Lasker should have patented this one

The German World Champion Emanuel Lasker played a perfect example of the Double Bishop Sacrifice in Amsterdam 1889. His game with Bauer has been the classic model for over 100 years.

It features a bishop sacrifice on h7, followed soon afterwards by a second bishop sacrifice on g7. The effect is to utterly demolish the protective pawn shelter in front of the black king. White can then attack down the g- and h-files with his major pieces. Black's king, denuded of shelter, will invariably perish if both White's queen and rook can enter the fray immediately.

Normally the white queen reaches the h-file swiftly, with a check. The critical issue is usually the speed with which the *white rook* can manoeuvre into the attack.

Typical Pattern for the Double Bishop Sacrifice

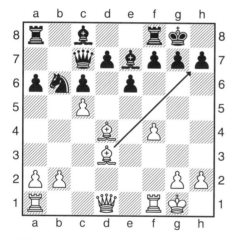

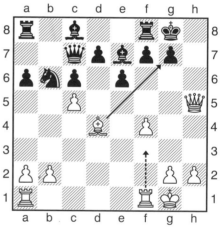

71a) White moves

The first bishop is sacrificed with 1 ♗xh7+ ♚xh7. Before making the second sacrifice, White brings his queen into the attack with check: 2 ♕h5+ ♚g8 *(71b)*.

71b) White moves

Now 3 ♗xg7 seriously exposes the black king. After 3...♚xg7 4 ♕g4+! ♚h8 White's rook enters the attack with 5 ♖f3, and mate with ♖h3+ follows.

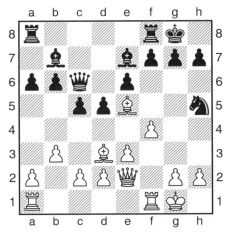

72a) White moves

This was the classic Lasker-Bauer game. After 1 ♗xh7+ ♚xh7 2 ♕xh5+ ♚g8 3 ♗xg7 ♚xg7 4 ♕g4+ ♚h7 5 ♖f3 Black tried the defence 5...e5 *(72b)*.

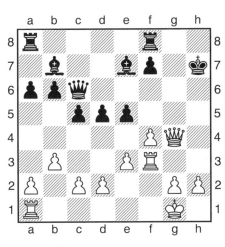

72b) White moves

Although Black avoided mate after 6 ♖h3+ ♕h6 7 ♖xh6+ ♚xh6, he lost on material following Lasker's 8 ♕d7!. The queen forks the two black bishops.

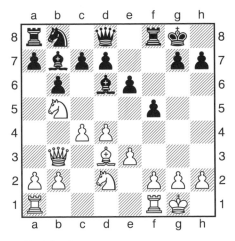

73) Black moves

After 1...♗xh2+ 2 ♚xh2 ♕h4+ 3 ♚g1 ♗xg2 the second bishop can be declined with 4 f3. But Black wins by 4...♕g3, preparing a discovered check.

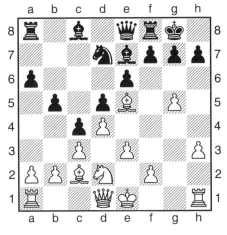

74) White moves

Even an obstructive pawn on g5 does not rule out the sacrifice: 1 ♗xh7+ ♚xh7 2 ♕h5+ ♚g8 3 ♗xg7 ♚xg7 4 ♕h6+ ♚g8 5 ♖g1! with ♖g4-h4 to follow.

47

DEADLY CHECKMATE 18

Morphy's Mate

A little R & B from Louisiana...

This theme is named after the legendary Paul Morphy from New Orleans (1837-84), because of a dazzling queen sacrifice he played against Louis Paulsen in 1857. The idea was to open the g-file, whereupon rook and bishop forced mate. You might wonder what is the difference from Pillsbury's Mate (Deadly Checkmate 19), where the winning concept is, well... basically the same! Over the years, no one has been prepared to choose between the two names. As there are lots of key themes, it suits our purpose to continue the little charade. In any case, both of these brilliant Morphy and Pillsbury combinations deserve to be honoured individually.

Morphy's Mate in the original form is rare. You are more likely get the *concealed* version. It is vital that White captures the black f7-pawn, before giving the final discovered check. Otherwise, when White's rook retreats along the g-file, Black could defend by advancing the pawn to f6.

Basic Pattern for Morphy's Concealed Mate

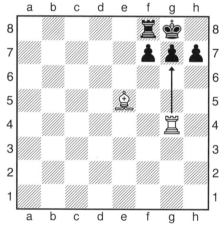

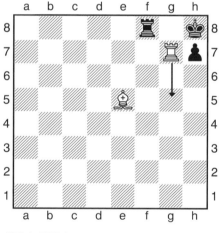

75a) White moves

After 1 ♖xg7+ ♔h8 White uses the discovered check (from his bishop) to capture the black f-pawn and repeat moves: 2 ♖xf7+! ♔g8 3 ♖g7+ ♔h8 *(75b)*.

75b) White moves

Having captured the black f-pawn, White is ready to give discovered check with any rook retreat on the g-file, e.g. 4 ♖g5+ ♖f6 5 ♗xf6 mate.

48

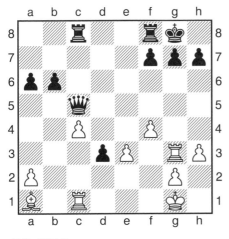

76) White moves

A perfect example of Morphy's Concealed Mate: 1 ♖xg7+ ♔h8 2 ♖xf7+ ♔g8 3 ♖g7+ ♔h8 4 ♖g3+, and mate follows shortly.

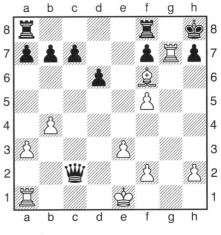

77) White moves

For a white bishop on f6, different rules apply. 1 ♗g5 mate is correct – but not 1 ♖xf7+? ♔g8 2 ♖g7+ ♔h8 3 ♖g5+? ♖xf6 and Black wins.

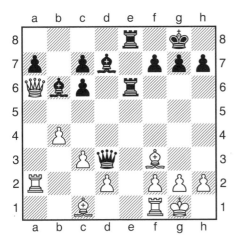

78a) Black moves

This is the Paulsen-Morphy game. Black played his famous queen sacrifice: 1...♕xf3! 2 gxf3 ♖g6+ 3 ♔h1 ♗h3 (*78b*) (threatening 4...♗g2+ 5 ♔g1 ♗xf3 mate).

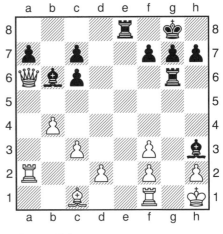

78b) White moves

After 4 ♖d1 ♗g2+ 5 ♔g1 ♗xf3+ 6 ♔f1 the quickest mate (Morphy played the slower 6...♗g2+) is 6...♖g2 7 ♕d3 ♖xf2+ 8 ♔g1 ♖g2+ 9 ♔h1 ♖g1.

Pillsbury's Mate

Rooked again on the g-file

The incredibly talented Harry Nelson Pillsbury (1872-1906) had more than one win with this concept, but his 16-move win over Lee in London 1899 was certainly the most amazing. In fact Pillsbury's Mate and Morphy's Mate (Deadly Checkmate 18) are really secret twins, but there are several different ways of checkmating using this pattern. For example, White's bishop could either start on the long diagonal (a1-h8) or on the h6-square. The key factor (with Black's king in its usual kingside castled position) is *the opening of the g-file* for the white rook.

White usually achieves this by either a straight capture of the black g7-pawn, by a sacrifice on g7, or by a sacrifice on the f6-square.

Typical Pattern for Pillsbury's Mate

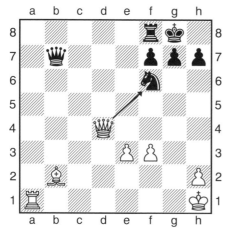

79a) White moves

The white queen is sacrificed with 1 ♕xf6 in order to open the g-file. After the recapture 1...gxf6, White continues with 2 ♖g1+ *(79b)*.

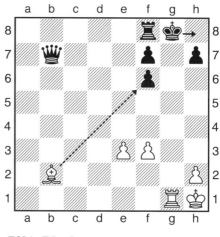

79b) Black moves

The black king is trapped in the crossfire of the white rook and bishop. After 2...♔h8, White plays 3 ♗xf6 checkmate.

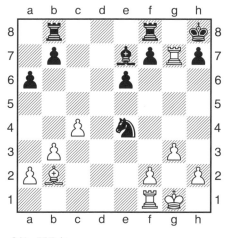

80) White moves

The motif *fails* if Black can interpose on the diagonal. After 1 ♖xf7+ ♗f6! 2 ♗xf6+ ♘xf6 Black remains knight for two pawns ahead.

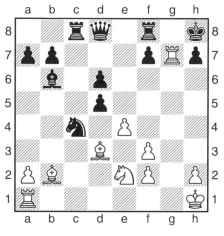

81) White moves

The usual discovered checks fail (as Black threatens ...♘xb2). But another motif emerges: 1 ♖g8++! (*double* check) 1...♔xg8 2 ♖g1+ ♕g5 3 ♖xg5 mate.

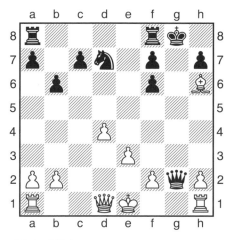

82a) White moves

This was the amazing Pillsbury-Lee game. The stunning sacrifice 1 ♕f3! deflects the black queen from the g-file. After 1...♕xf3 White plays 2 ♖g1+ *(82b)*.

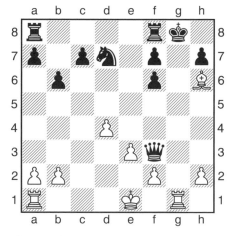

82b) Black moves

2...♔h8 is forced, when 3 ♗g7+ ♔g8 4 ♗xf6+ forces mate next move. A perfect illustration of the mate when White's bishop starts on the h6-square.

DEADLY CHECKMATE 20

The Crafty ♗g8

A gimmick that sometimes wins on the spot

In the course of a kingside attack, a white bishop often ends up on the h7-square. Usually the bishop has earlier given check, forcing the black king to the h8-square.

Occasionally, however, such a bishop can find itself impeding White's subsequent attack.

This commonly comes about when the white queen is poised to deliver checkmate on h7 – but can't because the bishop is in the way. When a bishop *retreat* will not solve the problem, you can consider a bizarre-looking *advance*. For this to work White *usually needs a second piece also covering the h7-square*, typically a knight on g5.

There is something rather sneaky about this theme, so don't expect your opponent to want to analyse afterwards!

Typical Pattern for the ♗g8 Trick

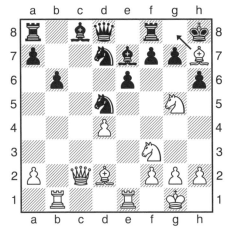

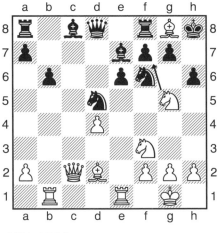

83a) White moves

1 ♗g8! clears the h7-square, and the bishop is temporarily immune from capture (due to the threat of 2 ♕h7 mate). Black replies 1...♘7f6 *(83b)*.

83b) White moves

Now 2 ♘xf7+ ♖xf7 3 ♗xf7 wins the exchange. Black avoided checkmate on h7, but not the *second threat* – the double attack on the square f7.

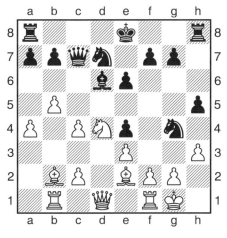

84a) Black moves

A typical scenario. First Black forces the white king into the corner by 1...♗h2+ 2 ♔h1. Then 2...♗g1! *(84b)* sets up the threat of mate with ...♕h2.

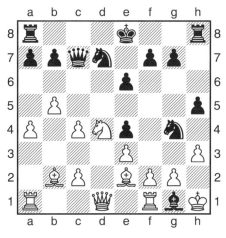

84b) White moves

The black queen's diagonal must be blocked. But on 3 g3, Black wins material by 3...♘xf2+ (forking the white king and queen, so White must capture) 4 ♖xf2 ♗xf2.

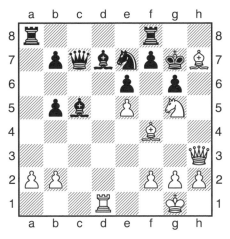

85) White moves

After 1 ♗g8 the white queen penetrates decisively to h7. For example 1...♖xg8 2 ♕h7+ ♔f8 3 ♕xf7 mate.

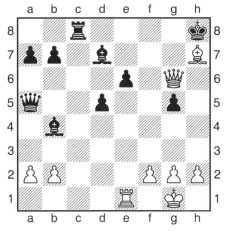

86) White moves

Here the queen and bishop alone can force mate. After 1 ♗g8 (threatening ♕h7) Black must capture with 1...♖xg8. White then mates by 2 ♕h6.

Rook Sacrifice on g7

Consider this possibility every move

If a white rook is attacking the black g7-pawn, *and the pawn is only protected by the black king*, then ♖xg7+ simply cries out to be played. If you have such a middlegame position, every time it is your turn to move you should ask yourself if such a sacrifice might now work.

For the sacrifice to be successful the other white attacking pieces – especially the queen – must be able to move in swiftly to exploit the exposed black king position.

Creating the initial situation, where the rook can pressure g7, is not that easy. White's own pawn on g2 usually blocks the g-file. Occasionally a rook can circumvent this by a transfer to the g3-square (perhaps via e3 or a3). However, putting a rook in front of your own g-pawn can be a rather artificial manoeuvre.

The most favourable version arises if the g-file is *semi-open* (i.e. White's g-pawn is missing). In this case *the second white rook can often also participate in the attack*.

Typical Pattern for the Rook Sacrifice on g7

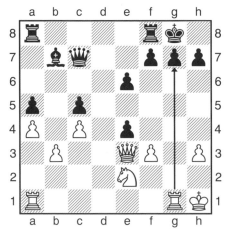

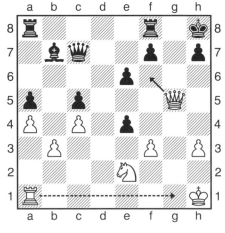

87a) White moves

The g-file is *semi-open* – and is thus a direct path leading to the black king. White plays 1 ♖xg7+ ♔xg7 2 ♕g5+! ♔h8 *(87b)*.

87b) White moves

After 3 ♕f6+ ♔g8 4 ♖g1+ the second white rook joins the attack, and mate follows next move. The queen zigzagging to f6 is a typical motif.

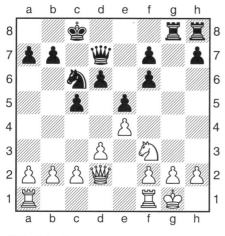

88) Black moves

After 1...♖xg2+ White will be poorly placed if he does not capture. But after 2 ♔xg2 comes 2...♕g4+ 3 ♔h1 ♕xf3+ 4 ♔g1 ♖g8+ 5 ♕g5 ♖xg5 checkmate.

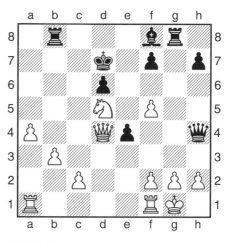

89) Black moves

The rook sacrifice can also save a difficult position. Here 1...♖xg2+ 2 ♔xg2 ♕g4+ 3 ♔h1 ♕f3+ 4 ♔g1 ♕g4+ gives a draw by perpetual check.

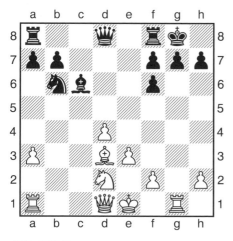

90) White moves

The g-file is semi-open – earlier Black unwisely snatched the g2-pawn with his bishop. After 1 ♖xg7+ ♔xg7 2 ♕g4+ ♔h8 3 ♕f5, mate on h7 follows.

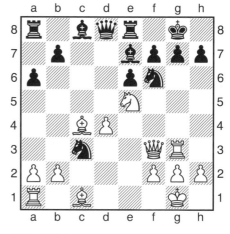

91) White moves

Here White's queen has back-up from several minor pieces. 1 ♖xg7+ ♔xg7 2 ♕g3+ wins after either 2...♔h8 3 ♘xf7 mate or 2...♔f8 3 ♗h6 mate.

DEADLY CHECKMATE 22

A Knight on f5 (1)

Double attacks don't get much better than this

A knight on the f5-square is beautifully posted for possible combinations involving the black king. It puts pressure on the g7-square, and, with Black's king in the standard castled position, can often threaten a decisive check on h6 or e7. It is particularly effective when teamed up with a white queen and dark-squared bishop,

One motif wins time and again if Black is careless. It comes about if *White's queen is able to utilize the g4-square*, and *Black's queen is undefended on the d7-square*. With the move ♕g4 (threatening ♕xg7 checkmate) White can often set up a devastating double attack. White threatens mate in one – and to win the enemy queen!

Black can attend to the mate threat, but then comes the knight check from White on h6, uncovering the discovered attack against the queen on d7. The combination in diagram 126b (Deadly Checkmate 29) also incorporates a lovely version of this theme.

Typical Pattern for the ♘f5/♕g4 Trap

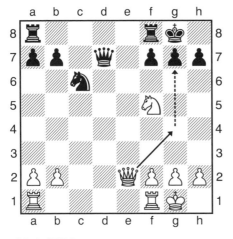

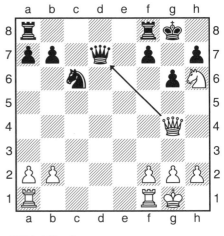

92a) White moves

With 1 ♕g4 White threatens immediate checkmate (by ♕xg7). Black must attend to the mate threat with 1...g6 (or 1...f6), but then comes 2 ♘h6+ *(92b)*.

92b) Black moves

The white knight on h6 is *giving check*, so the black king must move. After 2...♔g7 White plays 3 ♕xd7, winning the black queen.

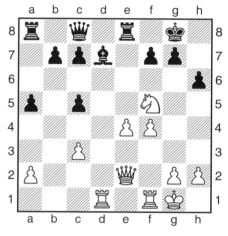

93) White moves

The exchange sacrifice 1 ♖xd7 ♕xd7 lures Black's queen to a fatal square. On 2 ♕g4 Black cannot cope with the double threat of 3 ♕xg7 mate and 3 ♘xh6+.

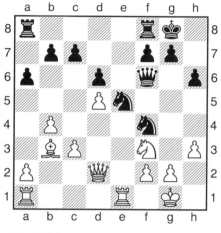

94) White moves

After 1 ♘xe5 White expected his opponent to recapture the knight. Instead Black played 1...♕g5! and White resigned, as he is mated or loses his queen.

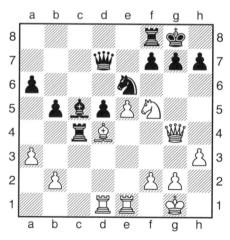

95) White moves

1 ♘xg7, winning a key black defensive pawn, exploits Black's unprotected queen on d7 in a different way (1...♘xg7? is met by 2 ♕xd7).

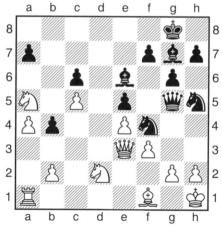

96) Black moves

Remarkably, White will lose his queen: 1...♘g3+! 2 hxg3 ♕h6+! (forcing the king to g1, so the next move is check) 3 ♔g1 ♘h3+ 4 gxh3 ♕xe3+.

DEADLY CHECKMATE **23**

A Knight on f5 (2)

Good knight, bad bishop

As already seen in Deadly Checkmate 22, a white knight on f5 is an aggressively placed piece. The pressure it exerts on the g7-square – directly in front of the castled black king – creates many possibilities. A typical attacking plan for White is to transfer the queen to the g-file (with either ♕g3, ♕g4 or ♕g5). Alternatively White can consider sacrificing a bishop on h6 to prise open the kingside.

One tactical point to bear in mind: *if Black has a bishop on e7 the combinational possibilities for White increase significantly.* The reason is that the bishop needs to be constantly guarded (against capture from the knight on f5). This can result in Black's defences being overloaded.

Typical Pattern with the Knight on f5

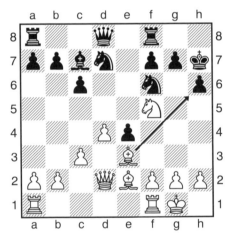

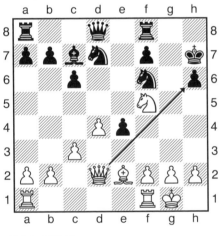

97a) White moves

With a knight on f5, the possibility of a bishop sacrifice on h6 is frequently present. White plays 1 ♗xh6, allowing the capture 1...gxh6 *(97b)*.

97b) White moves

The queen follows up the attack on the diagonal with 2 ♕xh6+. After the forced black king retreat, 2...♔g8, White plays 3 ♕g7 checkmate.

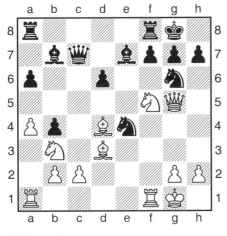

98) White moves

The winning queen sacrifice 1 ♕h6! threatens checkmate on g7. 1...gxh6 fails to 2 ♘xh6 mate and 1...♗f6 makes no difference after 2 ♗xf6.

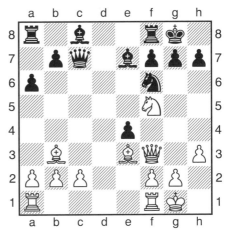

99) White moves

After 1 ♕g3 (threatening ♕xg7 mate *and* Black's queen on c7) 1...♕xg3 2 ♘xe7+! ♔h8 3 fxg3 White has won the bishop on e7 for nothing.

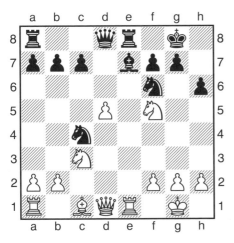

100) White moves

A subtle example of the double attack. White gains an advantage with 1 ♗xh6 gxh6 2 ♕d3, threatening 3 ♕xc4 and mate beginning with 3 ♕g3+.

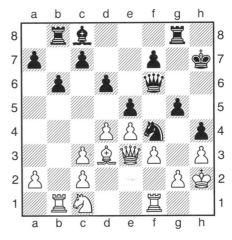

101) Black moves

1...♗xh3 2 gxh3 ♕e6 leaves White helpless, in spite of his having the move. After 3 ♔g1 ♕xh3 4 ♖f2 g4 the black attack will crash through.

Rook Decoy Sacrifice on h7

An open h-file is no place for a king

This theme usually involves all of the attacker's major pieces – the queen and both rooks. No surprise, then, that it is so often fatal for the defender. A danger-signal for Black (apart from an open or semi-open h-file) comes when the f7-point is attacked by White's queen and defended only by Black's king. The combination comprises three stages:

1) A white rook is sacrificed on h7, forcibly decoying Black's king to the h-file.

2) Once the king leaves the defence of f7, White's queen swoops in and gives check.

3) Black deals with the queen check, but his king remains trapped. White's remaining rook delivers checkmate on the h-file.

Typical Pattern for the Rook Decoy on h7

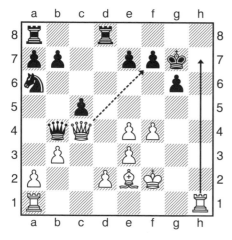

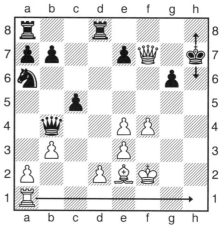

102a) White moves

1 ♖h7+ decoys the black king from the defence of the pawn on f7 – and onto the h-file. After 1...♔xh7 White's queen penetrates with 2 ♕xf7+ *(102b)*.

102b) Black moves

Although the black king can move with either 2...♔h6 or 2...♔h8, it remains trapped on the h-file. Next move White checkmates with 3 ♖h1.

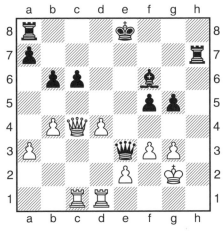

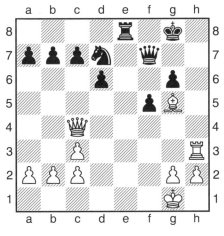

103) Black moves

The decoy may be possible *even if the second rook is not instantly available*. 1...♖h2+ 2 ♔xh2 ♕f2+ 3 ♔h1 ♔e7! wins in view of 4...♖h8+ next move.

104) White moves

Here the black pieces are unfortunately placed. White uses the rook deflection to win the queen with 1 ♖h8+ ♔g7 2 ♖h7+ ♔xh7 3 ♕xf7+.

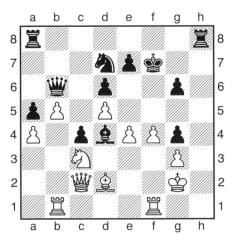

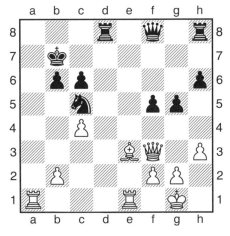

105) Black moves

A familiar theme, but with a highly original first move: 1...♗g1! (threatening ...♖h2 mate) 2 ♖xg1 ♖h2+ 3 ♔xh2 ♕f2+, and 4...♖h8 will mate next move.

106) White moves

1 ♖a7+ ♔xa7 2 ♕xc6 is not immediate mate, but Black's king will perish soon on the a-file: 2...♖b8 3 ♖a1+ ♘a6 4 ♕c7+ ♖b7 5 ♗xb6+ ♔a8 6 ♖xa6+.

The Queen and Bishop Mate

Don't under-rate this basic mate

A queen and a bishop are a classy double-act when it comes to homing in on the vulnerable h7-square. This straightforward but lethal mating pattern is fundamental to the success of many more complex combinations. The key components are a black king on h8, a white queen on the h-file, and a white bishop on h7. A move from the white bishop will unveil a discovered check from the queen.

White's mating plan involves retreating his bishop, giving the discovered check. After Black's king moves, White's queen will advance to h7-square, giving at least a check and frequently mate.

Basic Pattern for the Queen & Bishop Mate

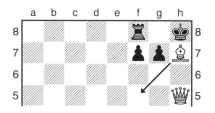

107a) White moves

The bishop retreats *anywhere* along the diagonal, uncovering a discovered check from White's queen. For example, 1 ♗f5+, forcing 1...♔g8 *(107b)*.

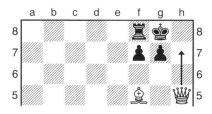

107b) White moves

2 ♕h7 is checkmate, as the white queen is supported by the bishop.

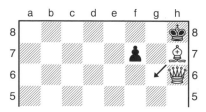

108a) White moves

Here White must be precise with the choice of retreat square for his bishop. Correct is 1 ♗g6+ ♔g8 *(108b)*.

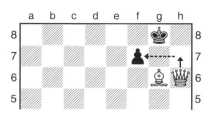

108b) White moves

After 2 ♕h7+ ♔f8 White can checkmate with 3 ♕xf7, as the queen *is supported by the bishop on g6*.

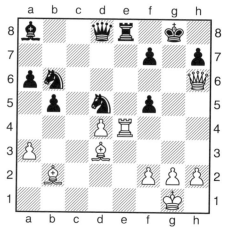

109) White moves

Here the standard formation is reached via a rook sacrifice: 1 ♖g4+ fxg4 2 ♗xh7+ ♔h8 3 ♗g6+ ♔g8 4 ♕h7+ ♔f8 5 ♕xf7 checkmate.

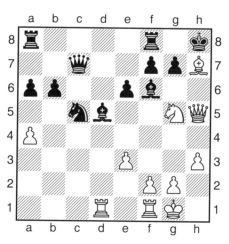

110) Black moves

On rare occasions Black has a defence. Here the saving move is 1...♗xg5, as White's discovered check (e.g. 2 ♗b1+) is blocked by 2...♗h6.

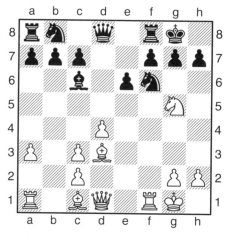

111a) White moves

First White makes a preliminary exchange sacrifice (of rook for knight) to eliminate the defender of the h7-square: 1 ♖xf6 ♕xf6 2 ♗xh7+ ♔h8 3 ♕h5 *(111b)*.

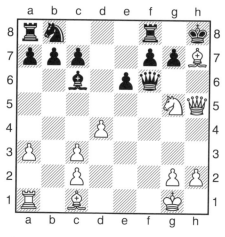

111b) Black moves

There is no defence to White's ♗g6+ and ♕h7 mate. 3...♖e8 fails to 4 ♘xf7+, 3...♕h6 to 4 ♘xf7+ ♖xf7 5 ♗xh6, and 3...g6 to 4 ♗xg6+ ♔g7 5 ♕h7 mate.

DEADLY CHECKMATE 26

Greco's Mate

A neat switchback

The attacking formation of a knight on g5, queen on h5 and bishop on c4 is very common. If Black has unwisely left insufficient pieces defending his kingside, the game can end very quickly. Here we deal with a particular manoeuvre whereby White's queen sneaks into the g6-square.

The term Greco's Mate was given to this manoeuvre in the book *The Art of Checkmate* (Renaud & Kahn), first published in English in 1953. Technically the name could apply to a wide range of positions where White opens the h-file by means of a knight sacrifice on the g-file. Gioacchino Greco (1600-c.1634) was an Italian chess writer, who published a number of ground-breaking manuals on the game.

Basic Pattern for Greco's Mate

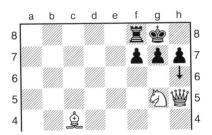

112a) Black moves

White's threat is ♕xh7 checkmate. To prevent this, Black plays 1...h6 *(112b)*, a move which also attacks the white knight.

112b) White moves

The f-pawn is captured with 2 ♗xf7+. Black replies 2...♔h8 *(112c)* (as 2...♖xf7 3 ♕xf7+ would cost rook for bishop).

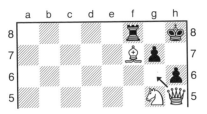

112c) White moves

Ignoring the attack on his knight, White plays 3 ♕g6. As checkmate on h7 is threatened, Black captures with 3...hxg5 *(112d)*.

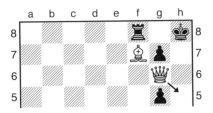

112d) White moves

Now that the h-file has been opened, the white queen returns: 4 ♕h5 checkmate. A neat switchback!

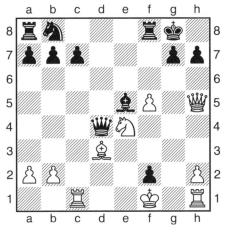

113) White moves

After 1 ♗c4+ ♚h8 the key elements of Greco's Mate appear. White continues 2 ♘g5 h6 3 ♕g6 (threatening mate on h7) 3...hxg5 4 ♕h5 checkmate.

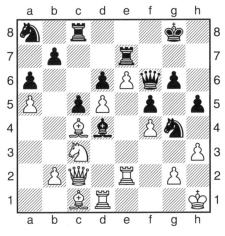

114) Black moves

Despite an extra defensive tempo (the pawn is already on h3) White is helpless after 1...♕h4, e.g. 2 ♖f1 ♕g3 3 hxg4 ♕h4 mate or 2 ♖d3 ♘f2+.

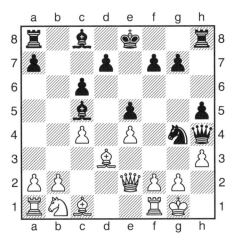

115a) Black moves

Here f2 is well defended by White, *but the black pawn on h5 means a related theme still works*. The knight is sacrificed with 1...♕g3 2 hxg4 hxg4 *(115b)*.

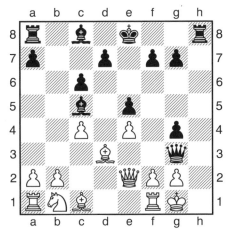

115b) White moves

3 ♖d1 avoids an instant mate, but there is no escape: 3...♕h2+ 4 ♚f1 ♕h1 checkmate. Again *the knight was sacrificed in order to open the h-file*.

DEADLY CHECKMATE 27

More ♕g6 Bombshells

The uninvited guest

A queen that penetrates to a weak square in the heart of enemy territory is always a danger for the defender. In this respect, the g6-square is one of the prime attacking outposts.

If the queen can reach the g6-square supported by two minor pieces, decisive combinations are frequently possible. One recurrent theme occurs when two white knights are able to move to the g5-square, enabling the queen to threaten mate on h7. Usually one knight is ready to be sacrificed, as the other will take its place.

Typical Pattern for Queen Supported by Two Knights

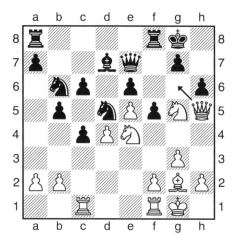

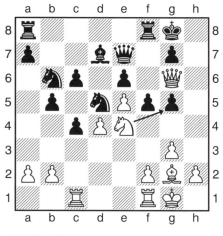

116a) White moves

1 ♕g6 sets up the threat of checkmate on h7. Black captures the white knight with 1...hxg5 *(116b)*, temporarily removing the threat.

116b) White moves

With 2 ♘xg5 the second white knight takes the place of its sacrificed colleague. The deadly threat of 3 ♕h7 mate is renewed.

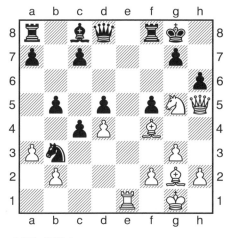

117) White moves

1 ♕g6 hxg5 2 ♗e5! wins, as Black has no good way to deal with the mate threat on g7. For example 2...♕d7 3 ♗xd5+ or 2...♖f7 3 ♗xg7 ♖xg7 4 ♖e8+.

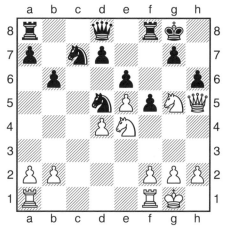

118) White moves

After 1 ♕g6 hxg5 2 ♘xg5 Black can avoid mate only by 2...♘f6 3 exf6 ♖xf6 4 ♕h7+ ♔f8 5 ♕h8+ ♔e7 6 ♕xg7+. White is a pawn up with an attack.

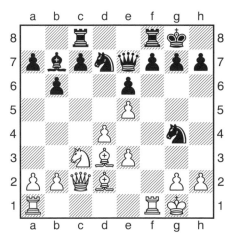

119a) Black moves

The queen manoeuvre is also potent in conjunction with a bishop on the long diagonal. Here 1...♕h4 forces 2 h3 (*119b*), due to the mate threat on h2.

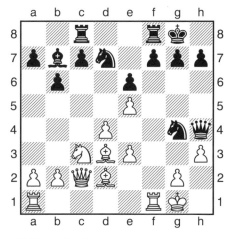

119b) Black moves

The continuation 2...♕g3 wins by *creating two mate threats simultaneously*. White cannot defend satisfactorily against both ...♕h2 and ...♕xg2.

DEADLY CHECKMATE 28   Korchnoi's Manoeuvre

Where did that queen come from?

The warning signs are there for Black, but easily overlooked:

1) *White has a bishop on the a2-g8 diagonal, pinning the black pawn on f7;*
2) *the white queen is somewhere on the b1-h7 diagonal; and*
3) *the black h-pawn has moved.*

The significance of the above three factors is that *the g6-square is probably available to the white queen.*

Bear in mind that the queen is a long-range piece, and is often innocently developed on the c2-square, with no evil intentions against the opposing king. It is understandable that its dramatic arrival in the heart of Black's kingside is not always anticipated by the defender!

This was the case when, as Black, Viktor Korchnoi played his crushing ...♕g3 move against Tatai in Beersheba 1978 (the position given immediately below).

Typical Pattern for Korchnoi's Manoeuvre

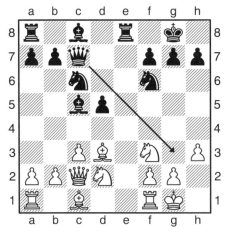

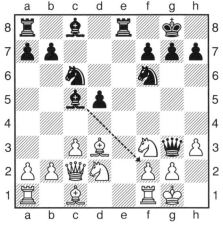

120a) Black moves

1...♕g3 *(120b)* exploits the fact that the white f-pawn is *pinned*. The black queen's unpleasant position forces White to deal with the threat of ...♗xh3.

120b) White moves

If 2 ♔h1, then Black wins a key pawn for nothing by 2...♗xf2. However, after 2 ♗f5, as played in the game, 2...♖e2 gives Black a powerful attack.

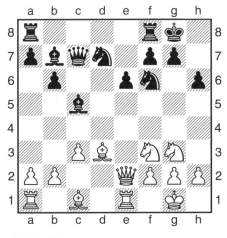

121) White moves

Losing a whole piece for nothing is a common blunder. Here White (an international strength player) played 1 h3?? and had to resign after 1...♕xg3.

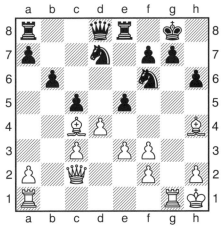

122) White moves

1 ♕g6 wins instantly, as there is no reasonable defence to the threat of 2 ♕xg7 mate. The queen cannot be captured, as the black f-pawn in pinned.

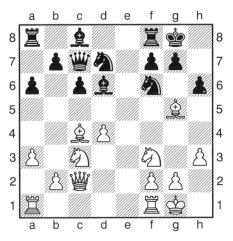

123a) White moves

The black h-pawn has just moved to h6. There follows 1 ♗xh6 ♘b6 (1...gxh6 loses to 2 ♕g6+ ♔h8 3 ♕xh6+ ♘h7 4 ♘g5 ♘f6 5 ♘ce4) 2 ♕g6 *(123b)*.

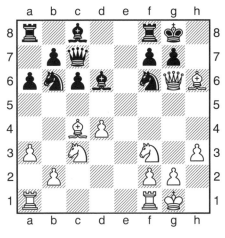

123b) Black moves

White's threat is ♕xg7 mate. After 2...♘e8 3 ♘g5, White's new threat of ♕h7 mate cannot be parried.

DEADLY CHECKMATE **29**

The ♗xh6 Sacrifice

A quickfire demolition that even wins in slow motion

The defensive move ...h6 by Black can be useful. In the long term Black's king has an escape hole against back-rank mates, and in the short term White's minor pieces are unable to utilize the square g5.

However, the pawn on h6 can also represent a target for the sacrifice of White's dark-squared bishop. If an immediate mate is impossible, a daring attacker can sacrifice on a medium-term basis provided the following conditions are met:

1) *White gains two pawns for the bishop, plus plenty of checks against the exposed black king; and*

2) *Black is tied up on the kingside, and unable to rearrange his defences whilst White brings reinforcements into the attack.*

These two factors can justify a bishop sacrifice where White takes several moves to manoeuvre an extra knight or rook to the kingside for the *coup de grâce*.

Typical pattern for the ♗xh6 sacrifice

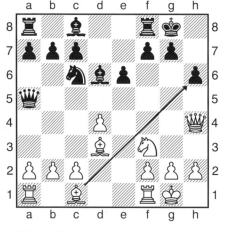

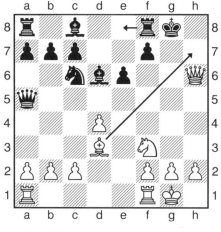

124a) White moves

In this straightforward version White wins immediately with 1 ♗xh6 gxh6 2 ♕xh6. The black king has been exposed, and the threat is mate with ♕h7.

124b) Black moves

There is no defence (as 2...f5 fails to 3 ♕g6+ ♔h8 4 ♘g5). If 2...♖e8 White mates with 3 ♗h7+ ♔h8 4 ♗g6+ ♔g8 5 ♕h7+ ♔f8 6 ♕xf7 mate.

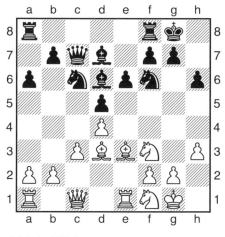

125a) White moves

The sacrifice 1 ♗xh6 gxh6 2 ♕xh6 ♗e7 *(125b)* does not give White immediate mate threats, but neither can Black bolster his critically weak kingside.

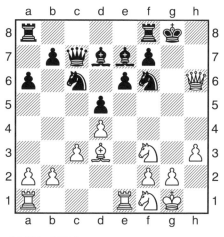

125b) White moves

There is even a choice of ways to feed extra white pieces into the attack, e.g. 3 ♘g3 and 3 ♖e3, or 3 ♘g5 e5 4 ♘g3 e4 5 ♘h5 ♘xh5 6 ♕h7 mate.

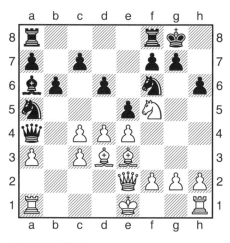

126a) White moves

Encouraged by the misplaced black pieces on the queenside, a superb kingside assault begins: 1 ♗xh6 gxh6 2 ♕e3 ♘e8 (2...♘g4 3 ♕h3) 3 ♕xh6 *(126b)*.

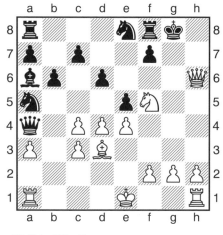

126b) Black moves

After 3...♕d7 (to stop ♘e7 mate) White exploits the loose queen brilliantly: 4 ♕g5+ ♔h7 5 ♕h4+ ♔g8 6 ♕g3+ ♔h8 7 ♕h3+ ♔g8 8 ♘h6+ ♔g7 9 ♕xd7.

The Queen & Bishop Line-up

The mate with no name (but countless victims)

Victims over the years must number in the tens of thousands, so it is surprising that this classic attacking formation has no title. Indeed, several standard openings are based around the manoeuvre. The white queen is placed on the b1-h7 diagonal (normally either on the c2- or d3-square) in front of the white bishop on the same diagonal. The effect of this simple manoeuvre is immediate. Mating possibilities directed against Black's vulnerable h7-square suddenly appear, as White's queen is supported in the attack by his bishop.

Whilst the queen and bishop line-up does not guarantee an advantage, it is worth setting up given the opportunity. The constant pressure against h7 can make Black's defence very unpleasant. One slip and it could be mate!

Basic Pattern for the Queen & Bishop Line-up

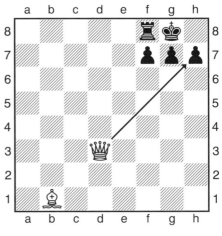

127a) White moves

With 1 ♗b1, followed by 2 ♕d3 (*127b*) next move, White rearranges his pieces so that the queen occupies the diagonal in front of the bishop.

127b) Black moves

The classic attacking formation. White's queen attacks the vulnerable h7-point, supported from behind by the bishop.

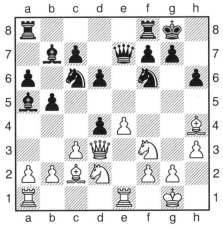

128) White moves

The pawn advance 1 e5 opens the key diagonal from d3 to h7 for the white queen. After 1...♘xe5 2 ♘xe5 dxe5 3 ♗xf6 ♕xf6 White checkmates with 4 ♕h7.

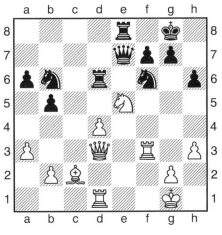

129) White moves

By eliminating the knight on f6 White can penetrate to h7 and gain a decisive attack: 1 ♖xf6 ♕xf6 2 ♕h7+ ♔f8 3 ♖f1 ♕e6 4 ♘g6+ and wins.

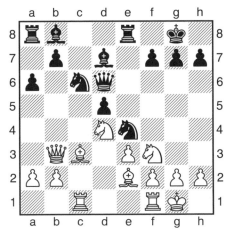

130) Black moves

Remarkably 1...♘xd4 wins a piece for Black, thanks to the line-up. If 2 exd4, then 2...♘xc3 3 ♖xc3 ♖xe2, and 2 ♗xd4 is worse due to 2...♘d2! 3 ♕d1 ♘xf3+ 4 ♗xf3 ♕xh2 mate.

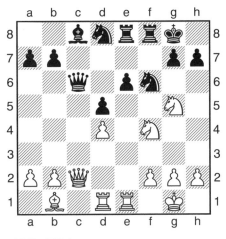

131) White moves

Here an unusual sacrifice followed by a semi-smothered mate foils Black's attempt to swap queens: 1 ♕xh7+ ♘xh7 2 ♗xh7+ ♔h8 3 ♘g6 checkmate.

Removing the f6 Defender

My kingdom for a horse!

A long-range piece can pressure weak points from afar. An example is a white queen developed on c2 or d3, which eyes Black's vulnerable h7-square. Add in just one other supporting piece (such as a white knight on g5 or a bishop on b1) and, potentially, White has sufficient firepower to checkmate with ♕xh7.

There remains one problem. In the standard castled position, Black normally has a knight developed on f6, protecting the h7-square. White could offer to exchange this defending knight, but this would alert Black to the danger, giving him time to stop the mate.

The trick is to attack the f6 knight *whilst simultaneously attacking another piece*, as Black will be unable to deal with both threats at once.

Typical Pattern for Removing the Knight on f6

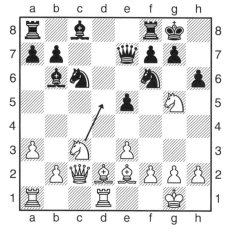

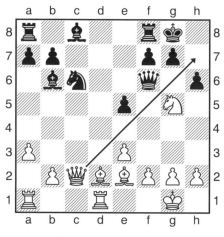

132a) White moves

1 ♘d5! simultaneously attacks Black's queen and the knight on f6. To avoid immediate loss the black queen must move (if 1...♘xd5, then 2 ♕h7 mate): 1...♕d8 2 ♘xf6+ ♕xf6 *(132b)*.

132b) White moves

There follows 3 ♕h7 checkmate. Note how the black knight on f6, the vital defender of h7, was eliminated by utilizing an attack on Black's queen.

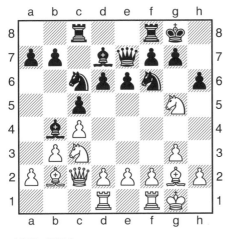

133) White moves

The white knight on g5 is attacked. Instead of retreating White eliminates the knight on f6 with a sacrifice: 1 ♘d5 exd5 2 ♗xf6 ♕xf6 3 ♕h7 mate.

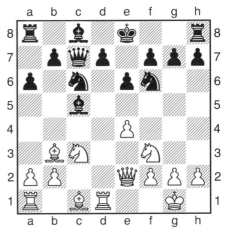

134) Black moves

An ordinary-looking position turns nasty for White after 1...♘g4 2 ♖f1? (defending the f2-pawn, but 2 ♗e3 was necessary) 2...♘d4! winning outright.

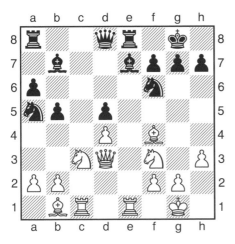

135a) White moves

1 ♗c7! is a spectacular decoy sacrifice. Now after 1...♕xc7 2 ♘xd5 (*135b*) Black's queen is attacked twice (by the knight on d5 and the rook on c1).

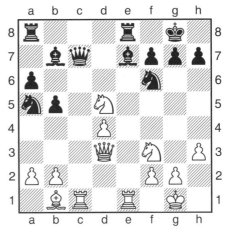

135b) Black moves

The black queen must be given up for insufficient compensation (with 2...♗xd5 3 ♖xc7), as 2...♕d8 allows mate by 3 ♘xf6+ ♗xf6 4 ♕xh7+ ♔f8 5 ♕h8.

DEADLY CHECKMATE 32

The Greek Gift (1)

Better to give a Greek Gift than receive one

The classic Greek Gift sacrifice may be the most dominant attacking theme in chess. Every year, thousands of bishops are sacrificed for unmoved h-pawns, in a myriad of different positions. The aim is always the same – to expose the enemy king, which has castled on the kingside. Whilst the defender usually has little choice but to accept the sacrifice, the subsequent attack is by no means always a forced win.

After White plays ♗xh7+, the classic follow-up is with the attacking moves ♘g5+ and ♕h5. Whether White's attack then succeeds or fails depends on the formation of each side's pieces *at that precise moment*. Therefore it is a huge advantage to know the most standard winning motifs.

Basic Pattern for the Greek Gift Sacrifice
(Black returns with the king to g8)

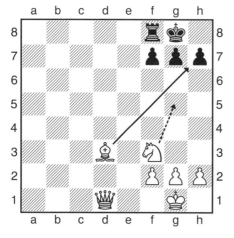

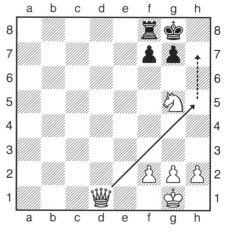

136a) White moves

With 1 ♗xh7+ the white bishop is sacrificed for the pawn on h7. After 1...♔xh7 2 ♘g5+ the black king retreats from the knight check with 2...♔g8 *(136b)*.

136b) White moves

The white queen advances with 3 ♕h5. Because the white knight is already on g5, 4 ♕h7 checkmate is threatened.

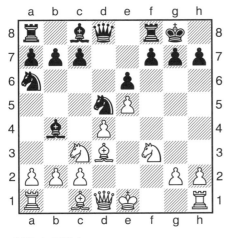

137a) White moves

On 1 ♗xh7+ ♔xh7 2 ♘g5+ Black cannot capture the knight with his queen, as White's bishop protects it. After 2...♔g8, 3 ♕h5 *(137b)* threatens mate.

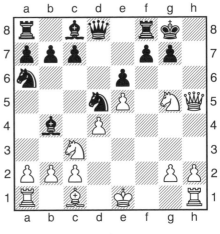

137b) Black moves

The f6-square *is unavailable to the black knight*, so 3...♖e8 is forced (to create an escape hole for the king). White continues with 4 ♕xf7+ ♔h8 *(137c)*.

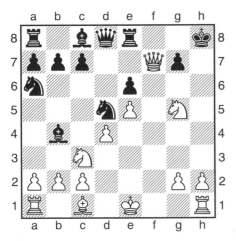

137c) White moves

The white queen keeps checking: 5 ♕h5+ ♔g8 6 ♕h7+ ♔f8 *(137d)*. Black has no time to arrange his defences, as he must respond to check every move.

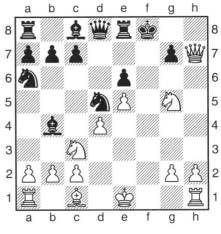

137d) White moves

Now it becomes clear why *the capture of the f7-pawn was interpolated*. After 7 ♕h8+ ♔e7, White gives checkmate with 8 ♕xg7.

The Greek Gift (2)

Come into my parlour...

After White's sacrifice of ♗xh7+, and check on g5 with the knight, Black can advance his king to g6. The idea of this defence is to stop White's powerful ♕h5, which would follow on the retreat ...♔g8.

However, the black king is potentially very exposed on the g6-square. In general White will win if he can bring reinforcements into the attack, although in some positions Black does escape with his extra piece.

It is vital to realize that White *does not always have an immediate forced win* against the ...♔g6 defence. The pressure against the black king can be medium-term. You may need to calmly manoeuvre extra pieces or pawns into the attack, almost ignoring the fact you are a piece down. A good test of character!

Typical Pattern for the Greek Gift Sacrifice
(Black tries the ...♔g6 defence)

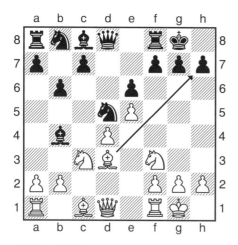

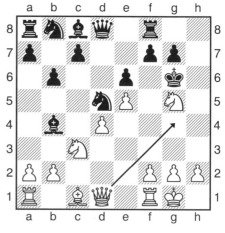

138a) White moves

After 1 ♗xh7+ ♔xh7 2 ♘g5+ the black king advances with 2...♔g6 *(138b)*. White must consider his follow-up: perhaps 3 ♕g4, 3 h4 or 3 ♕d3+.

138b) White moves

3 ♕g4 is the most common attacking continuation. A lethal discovered check is looming (4 ♘xe6+) and 3...f5 4 ♕g3 maintains the threat.

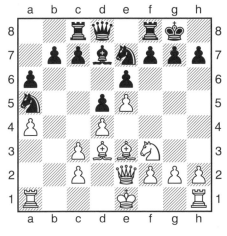

139a) White moves

After 1 ♗xh7+ ♚xh7 2 ♘g5+ ♚g6 (139b) the continuation 3 ♕g4 would not be so clear. Black has the reply 3...f5, and then 4 exf6 ♚xf6 or 4 ♕g3 f4 5 ♕g4 ♕e8.

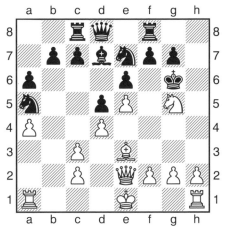

139b) White moves

Instead of 3 ♕g4, White plays 3 h4! winning easily. The threat of 4 h5+ next move is very strong, as Black's king will be driven into the centre.

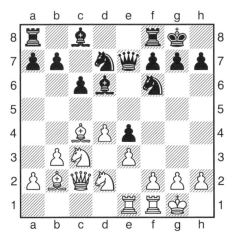

140) Black moves

Here the sacrifice is tempting but not correct. If 1...♗xh2+, then 2 ♚xh2 ♘g4+ 3 ♚g3 and now 3...♕g5 4 ♘dxe4 ♕g6 5 ♚f3, or 3...♕d6+ 4 f4 exf3+ 5 ♚xf3.

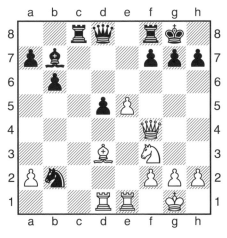

141) White moves

1 ♗xh7+ ♚xh7 2 ♘g5+ ♚g6 3 h4! gives White a dangerous attack, for example 3...♘xd1 4 h5+ ♚xh5 5 g4+ ♚g6 6 ♕f5+ ♚h6 7 ♘xf7+ ♖xf7 8 ♕h5 mate.

The Greek Gift (3)

A king on h6 in the middlegame?

The defence of ...♚h6 in answer to the Greek Gift bishop sacrifice has the same idea as the ...♚g6 defence (Deadly Checkmate 33). But the ...♚h6 defence is rarer, because the black king is usually more exposed. For example, if White has a dark-squared bishop on the c1-h6 diagonal, there is already a potential discovered check.

Another downside is that *White's queen can often administer an unpleasant check on the h-file*.

Therefore ...♚h6 is only a serious defence in positions where White has advanced a pawn to h4. The reason is that this pawn shields the black king from queen checks on the h-file.

**Typical Pattern for the Greek Gift Sacrifice
(Black tries the ...♚h6 defence)**

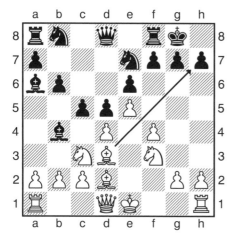

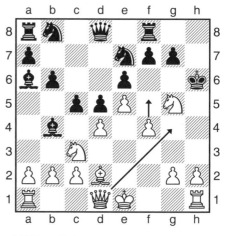

142a) White moves

1 ♗xh7+ ♚xh7 2 ♘g5+ ♚h6 *(142b)* and, in this favourable version, White has a choice of wins, e.g. 3 f5 prepares a discovered check from the d2-bishop.

142b) White moves

Another win is 3 ♕g4, threatening mate in two by checking with the queen on the h-file. For example, 3...♘f5 4 ♕h3+ ♚g6 5 ♕h7 checkmate.

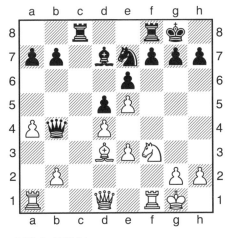

143a) White moves

The white dark-squared bishop is absent, but 1 ♗xh7+ ♚xh7 2 ♘g5+ ♚h6 3 ♕g4 still gives a strong attack. Black's 3...♕d2 *(143b)* attacks the e3-pawn.

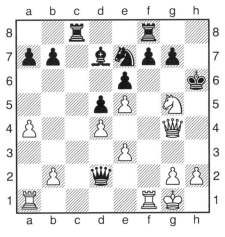

143b) White moves

A typical Greek Gift king-hunt begins: 4 ♕h4+ ♚g6 5 ♕h7+ ♚xg5 6 h4+ ♚g4 7 ♕xg7+ ♘g6 8 ♕h6 ♘xh4 9 ♖f4+ ♚g3 10 ♕xh4 checkmate.

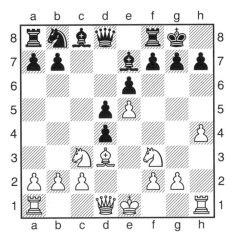

144a) White moves

Here the presence of the white pawn on h4 encourages Black to try the ...♚h6 defence: 1 ♗xh7+ ♚xh7 2 ♘g5+ ♚h6!? *(144b)*.

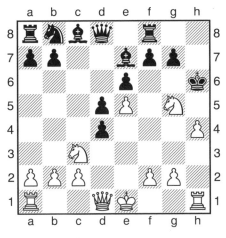

144b) White moves

There is no instant win, as White cannot arrange a queen check on the h-file. 3 ♕d3 (threatening ♕h7 mate) 3...g6 4 h5!? gives a very unclear position.

DEADLY CHECKMATE **35** The Greek Gift (4)

Re-writing the classics...

There are so many different positions where the classic Greek Gift sacrifice can be played that an entire book could be written on the subject. The attack can also fail immediately; for example, if Black is able to defend the h7-square after White's ♛h5. A black knight moving to f6, or a black bishop to f5 would achieve this.

On the other hand, there are some sophisticated versions (such as with a white pawn on h4 and rook on h1) where White wins even though Black can eliminate the attacking knight on g5.

Typical Pattern for the Greek Gift Sacrifice (advanced version)

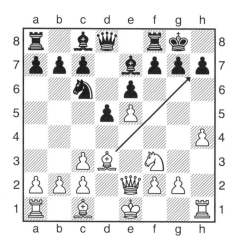

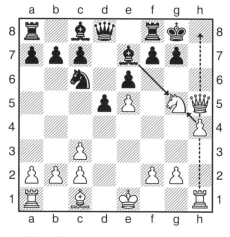

145a) White moves

Despite the defending black bishop on e7, the sacrifice works *thanks to White's pawn on h4 and rook on h1*. 1 ♗xh7+ ♚xh7 2 ♘g5+ ♚g8 3 ♛h5 *(145b)*.

145b) Black moves

The bishop can capture the knight, but 3...♗xg5 4 hxg5 *opens the h-file for White's rook*. Then after 4...f6 5 g6 Black cannot avoid mate on h7 or h8.

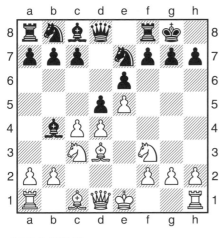

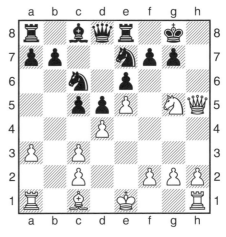

146a) White moves

A fine example *where Black has a knight on e7*. After 1 ♗xh7+ ♔xh7 2 ♘g5+ ♔g8 3 ♕h5 ♖e8 *(146b)* White turns down the 'free offer' of the f7-pawn.

146b) White moves

4 ♕h7+! is correct (since after 4 ♕xf7+ ♔h8 5 ♕h5+ ♔g8 Black's king can later escape via f7). After 4...♔f8 5 ♕h8+ ♘g8 6 ♘h7+ ♔e7 7 ♗g5+ White wins.

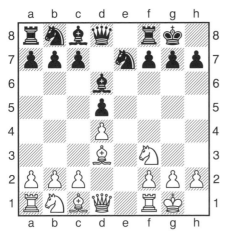

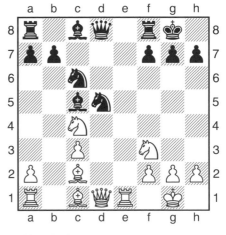

147) White moves

The sacrifice is *not* playable here *as Black's bishop can reach the b1-h7 diagonal*. If 1 ♗xh7+ ♔xh7 2 ♘g5+ ♔g8 3 ♕h5, then 3...♗f5 defends the h7-square.

148) White moves

The sacrifice is *not* playable here *as Black's knight can move to f6*. If 1 ♗xh7+ ♔xh7 2 ♘g5+ ♔g8 3 ♕h5, then 3...♘f6 defends the h7-square.

DEADLY CHECKMATE 36 — Mate on the Long Diagonal

A dangerous highway

A dark-squared bishop that controls the long diagonal, from a1 to h8, generates many combinational possibilities. It also cooperates well with all of the other pieces. An attack down the h-file with rooks is enhanced, for example, as the bishop controls the h8-square.

A double-act of bishop and queen is particularly virulent. By lining up the queen on the long diagonal, in front of the bishop, White can threaten mate on the g7- and h8-squares. Even if mate is preventable, Black can rather easily drop a stray piece to a queen fork that threatens mate in one at the same time.

Typical Pattern for Mate on the Long Diagonal

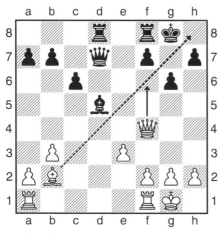

149a) White moves

The white bishop, raking the long diagonal, controls the g7- and h8-squares right next to the black king. White exploits the weakness with 1 ♕f6 *(149b)*.

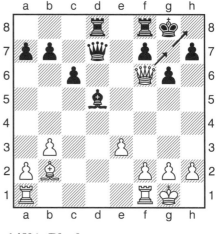

149b) Black moves

The weak dark squares render Black helpless. There is no way to stop White giving checkmate next move with either 2 ♕g7 or 2 ♕h8.

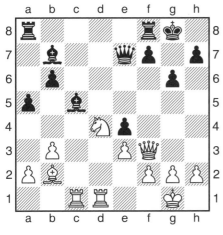

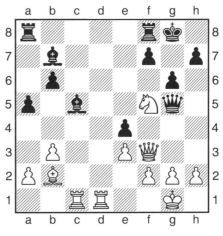

150a) White moves

Ignoring the attack on his queen, White plays 1 ♘f5 (threatening ♘h6 mate and ♘xe7+). Black cannot capture (1...gxf5 2 ♕g3+) and replies 1...♕g5 *(150b)*.

150b) White moves

The sacrifice 2 ♘h6+ ♕xh6 deflects the black queen. White then wins with 3 ♕f6, setting up a lethal mating pattern on the long diagonal.

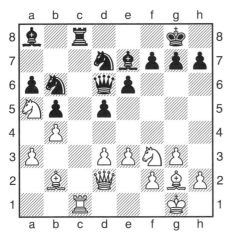

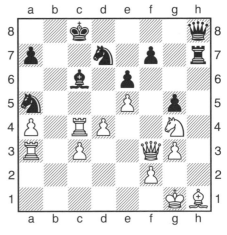

151) White moves

The two-move combination 1 ♖xc8+ ♘xc8 2 ♕c3 wins a piece due to a double attack. White threatens both the knight on c8 and a mate on g7.

152) Black moves

1...♖xh1+ 2 ♕xh1 ♕xh1 mate illustrates an 'X-ray attack'. The power of Black's bishop is felt right through the white queen to the h1-square.

Weak Dark Squares

The unfortunate case of the missing fianchettoed bishop

Weak dark squares arise when the black g-pawn has moved to g6, *but Black does not have a fianchettoed bishop on g7*. The absence of this protective bishop means that it is much easier for White to utilize the squares f6 and h6 for an attack. Furthermore the g7 and h8 dark squares, next to the castled black king, are potential mating spots.

Four positional methods of exploiting weak dark squares are:

1) *marching a white pawn to f6 or h6; or*
2) *bringing a white bishop to f6 or h6.*

A bishop or pawn lodged on either h6 or f6 is particularly dangerous if the white queen is able to enter the attack.

Basic Patterns for Mate on the Dark Squares

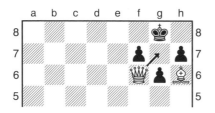

153) White moves

1 ♕g7 is checkmate. The white queen is protected by the bishop on h6.

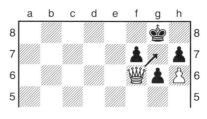

154) White moves

1 ♕g7 is checkmate. The queen is protected by the pawn on h6.

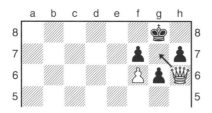

155) White moves

1 ♕g7 is checkmate. The queen is protected by the pawn on f6.

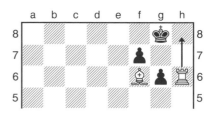

156) White moves

1 ♖h8 is checkmate. A bishop posted on f6 provides a wide range of mating possibilities.

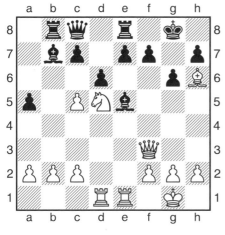

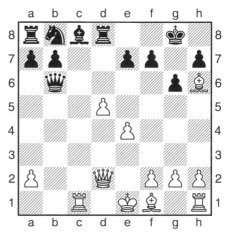

157) White moves

Both the black bishop on e5 and black e7-pawn are eliminated so that White can use the f6-square: 1 ♖xe5 dxe5 2 ♘xe7+ ♖xe7 3 ♕f6 and wins.

158) White moves

A bishop on h6 also assists in back-rank mates. 1 ♕c3 threatens mate on the g7-square. On 1...f6 there follows 2 ♕xc8 ♖xc8 3 ♖xc8+ ♔f7 4 ♖f8 mate.

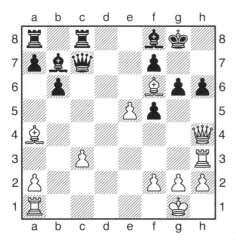

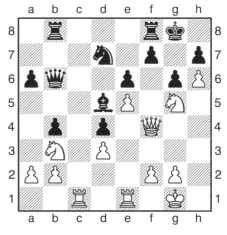

159) White moves

After 1 ♕xh6 ♗xh6 2 ♖xh6, checkmate (with ♖h8) cannot be prevented. A master would recognize this very commonplace pattern instantly.

160) White moves

White's queen would love to go to the f6-square (to threaten ♕g7 mate). So the black knight is decoyed with 1 ♘c5! ♘xc5 2 ♕f6 and mate will follow.

DEADLY CHECKMATE 38 Blackburne's Other Mate

Give Dad a fright with bishop & knight

A bishop and knight cooperate well to exploit weak dark squares. A pretty example was the game Albin-Blackburne in 1897, where Blackburne won in only 17 moves.

A white bishop on the long diagonal a1-h8 can be unpleasant for Black if the diagonal is not blocked by any pieces or pawns. Even stationed on the distant posts a1 or b2, the bishop exerts real pressure on the black king position. This is especially the case if:

a) *Black's own dark-squared bishop is absent; and*

b) *the black g7-pawn has moved or is missing.*

To exploit such a favourable position, if possible manoeuvre one of your knights to a light square (such as f5 or g4) near the black king.

Basic Patterns for Blackburne's Other Mate

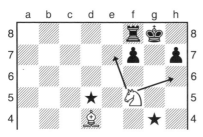

161) White moves

Both 1 ♘h6 and 1 ♘e7 give checkmate. The squares d5 and g4 (marked '★') are also fine outposts for the white knight.

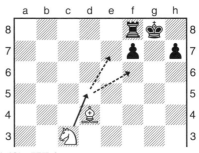

162) White moves

1 ♘d5 threatens mate next move with 2 ♘e7, and also an unpleasant check on the f6-square.

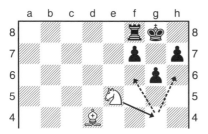

163) White moves

1 ♘g4 is frequently a powerful manoeuvre. From g4 the knight threatens both mate on h6 and a dangerous check on f6.

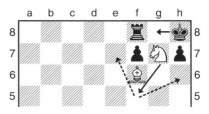

164) White moves

A typical mating-net arises after 1 ♘f5+ ♔g8. Both 2 ♘h6 and 2 ♘e7 are checkmate.

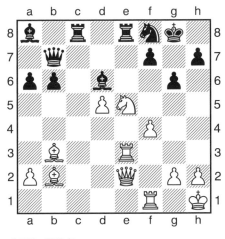

165) White moves

1 ♘g4 wins by exploiting the *weak dark squares* around Black's king. In addition to 2 ♘h6 checkmate, White threatens 2 ♖xe8 and 2 ♘f6+.

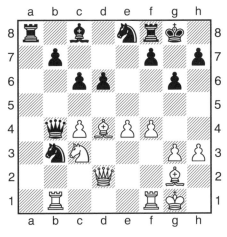

166) White moves

The spectacular 1 ♘d5! (threatening mate by 2 ♘e7) leaves Black no time to capture the white queen. After 1...cxd5 2 ♕xb4 White wins.

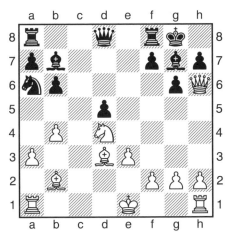

167) White moves

The fianchettoed black bishop defending the dark squares is summarily removed: 1 ♕xg7+ ♔xg7 2 ♘f5++ (*double check!*) 2...♔g8 3 ♘h6 mate.

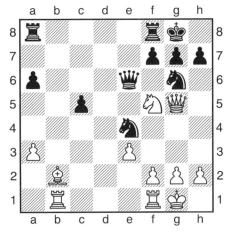

168) White moves

A surprising but not uncommon manoeuvre wins in one move. 1 ♕h6! threatens unstoppable mate on g7, as on 1...gxh6 comes 2 ♘xh6 mate.

DEADLY CHECKMATE 39

Lolli's Mates

One little pawn... one big heap of trouble

Advancing the f-pawn to soften up the enemy king position can be a powerful manoeuvre, given the right circumstances. Once lodged on the f6-square, the pawn will be a mighty thorn in Black's side. Some of the threats – such as back-rank mate possibilities – can persist into the endgame.

The situation is extremely dangerous for the defender if there is also a white queen in the vicinity of the black king. Although immediate mate on g7 may be avoided, *Black's defences generally crumble if White can introduce a further rook or knight into the attack*. The mate with the rook is named after the Italian chess scribe Giambattista Lolli (1698-1769).

Basic Pattern with the Pawn on f6

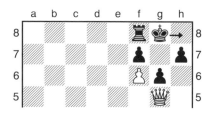

169a) Black moves

To counter White's checkmate threat (of ♕h6 followed by ♕g7) Black plays 1...♔h8 *(169b)*.

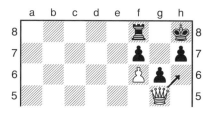

169b) White moves

The white queen advances with 2 ♕h6 *(169c)*, threatening checkmate on the g7-square.

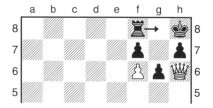

169c) Black moves

1...♖g8 *(169d)* prevents the checkmate, *but blocks g8 – a potential escape square for Black's king.*

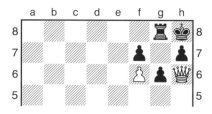

169d) White moves

By bringing either *a knight to g5*, or *a rook to the h-file*, White will very likely win immediately.

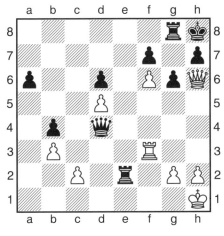

170) White moves

A rook down, and facing mate himself, White nevertheless wins using the Lolli queen sacrifice: 1 ♕xh7+ ♔xh7 2 ♖h3+ ♕h4 3 ♖xh4 mate.

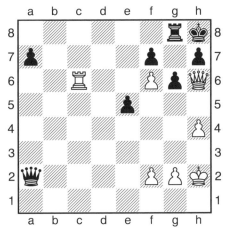

171) White moves

After 1 ♖c8, Black cannot prevent checkmate next move by 2 ♕g7.

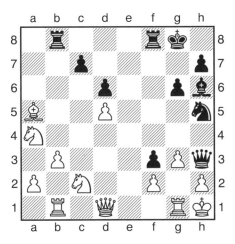

172) Black moves

1...♘f6 2 ♕f1 ♘g4! 3 ♕xh3 ♘xf2 is a pretty semi-smothered mate. Neither is 2 ♕xf3 a defence, on account of 2...♘g4 3 ♕g2 ♘xf2+.

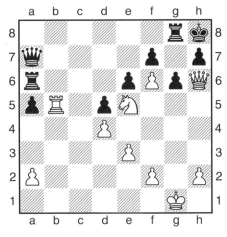

173) White moves

The sacrifice 1 ♖b8! wittily illustrates both the knight and rook motifs combined. 1...♖xb8 allows 2 ♕g7 mate, and 1...♕xb8 fails to 2 ♘xf7 mate.

DEADLY CHECKMATE **40**

Back-Rank Mates

Where Dad's own pawns are unwitting accomplices

This is possibly the most frequently encountered theme of all. The standard back-rank mate occurs when a queen or rook gives check on the eighth rank, and *the opposing king's escape is prevented by his own pawns.* Usually this involves the formation with three black pawns lined up in front of the castled king. In the early middlegame, this row of pawns (on f7, g7 and h7) is an excellent shield for Black's king from a *frontal attack*. But later, as pawns elsewhere on the board are exchanged, files open up, and the chances escalate that a queen or rook might penetrate to the back rank. Suddenly the protective wall of pawns turns into a death trap.

To avoid getting 'back-rank mated' yourself, consider making a precautionary 'hole' for your king after castling (e.g. by pushing the h-pawn one square).

Typical Pattern for the Back-Rank Mate

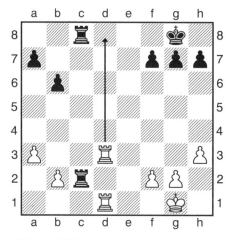

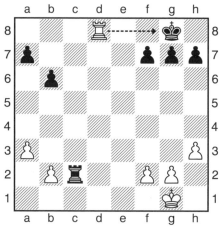

174a) White moves

As Black has omitted to 'make air' for his king, White plays 1 ♖d8+ ♖xd8 2 ♖xd8 checkmate *(174b).*

174b) Black is checkmated

Note how Black's king is hemmed in by his own three kingside pawns, and cannot escape the check from White's rook.

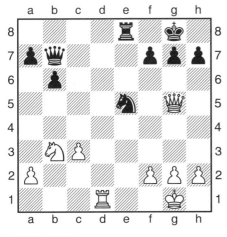

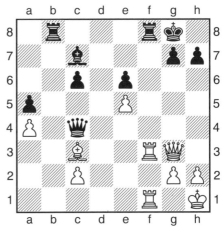

175) White moves

1 ♕xe5 wins a piece – a typical way to exploit the possibility of back-rank mate. If 1...♖xe5 White checkmates with 2 ♖d8+ ♖e8 3 ♖xe8.

176) Black moves

With the white king in the corner, just two pawns (on g2 and h2) are enough to block the king's escape. Black mates with 1...♕xf1+ 2 ♖xf1 ♖xf1.

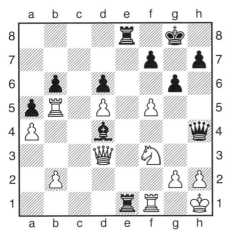

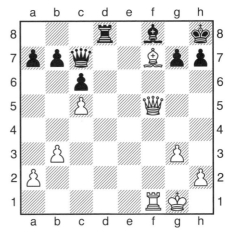

177) Black moves

The thematic manoeuvre 1...♕f2 ends the game, due to White's weak back rank. For example, 2 ♘xe1 ♖xe1 3 ♖xe1 ♕xe1+ 4 ♕f1 ♕xf1 mate.

178) White moves

After the startling 1 ♗e8! the back-rank mate threats decide. On 1...♗e7 comes 2 ♕f8+, whilst 1...♖xe8 similarly fails to 2 ♕xf8+ ♖xf8 3 ♖xf8 mate.

93

The Refined Back-Rank Mate

A back-rank mate with a touch of class

In this lovely variation on the standard back-rank mate, White makes a preliminary sacrifice to *decoy the sole piece defending the back-rank*. In the vast majority of cases the sacrifice is made on the f7-square, and the defending piece involved is a black rook on the f8-square.

Although any piece can act as the decoy, capturing with the queen on f7 (giving check and attacking the black rook) is clearly the most devastating version. There are two basic patterns to look out for. In one the queen is supported by a white bishop and rook. In the other (taking one move longer) two rooks provide the back-up.

Typical Pattern for the Refined Back-Rank Mate

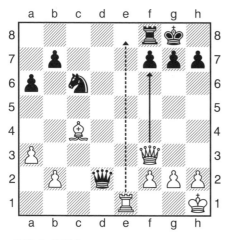

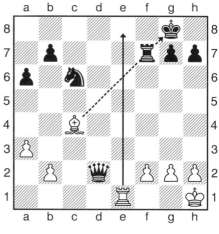

179a) White moves

If the black rook were absent, White could give a back-rank mate with his own rook. There follows the decoy sacrifice 1 ♕xf7+, forcing 1...♖xf7 *(179b)*.

179b) White moves

2 ♖e8 gives checkmate on the back rank. The black rook cannot interpose as it is pinned by the white bishop on c4.

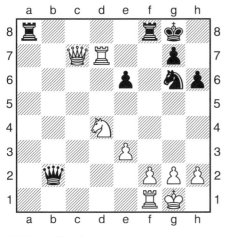

180a) Black moves

Tricking your opponent from a lost position is called a 'swindle' – and this is an example! After 1...♕xf2+ White must capture with 2 ♖xf2.

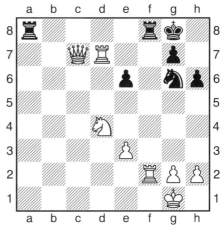

180b) Black moves

After 1...♖a1+ Black's sneaky idea is revealed. The white rook can interpose with 2 ♖f1, but Black mates with a capture on f1 by either rook.

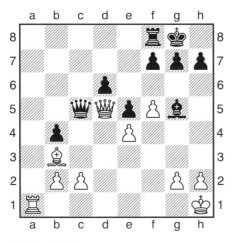

181) White moves

The white queen can come from almost anywhere to sacrifice on f7; this version is easily missed by Black. 1 ♕xf7+ ♖xf7 2 ♖a8+ and mate follows.

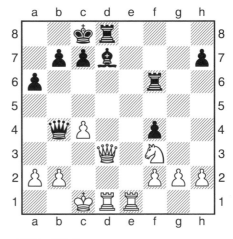

182) White moves

The queenside is a much rarer setting, but the refined back-rank mate is still possible. White plays 1 ♕xd7+ ♖xd7 2 ♖e8+ ♖d8 3 ♖(either)xd8 mate.

DEADLY CHECKMATE 42 — More Back-Rank Mates

*Learning the danger signals will win you
– and save you – many games*

In the standard back-rank mate (Deadly Checkmate 40) Black's king was fatally hemmed in by his own three unmoved kingside pawns. When the white rook or queen checked on the eighth rank, the unfortunate king had no escape.

There are dozens of variations on this pattern, as even if one or more of the defending pawns has moved (or is absent), a mate on the back rank is still possible.

This occurs when the *potential escape route for the king is controlled by enemy white pieces or pawns.*

Basic Pattern for the Back-Rank Mate
(where Black has a fianchettoed bishop)

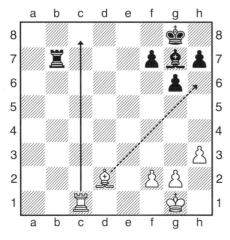

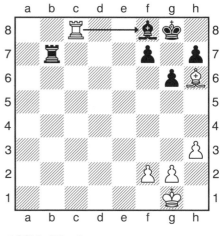

183a) White moves

After 1 ♖c8+ ♗f8 2 ♗h6 (*183b*) the black king cannot escape via g7, as this square is now controlled by the white bishop.

183b) Black moves

Although having the move, Black is lost. There is no defence to White's threat of ♖xf8 checkmate.

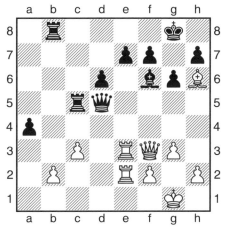

184) White moves

The danger signal here is the bishop on h6, which prevents Black's king advancing off the back rank. White plays 1 ♕xf6 exf6 2 ♖e8+ ♖xe8 3 ♖xe8 mate.

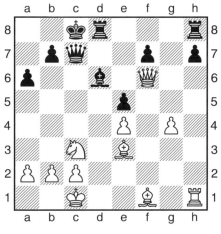

185) Black moves

Here Black can capture a knight with impunity by 1...♕xc3. A back-rank mate would follow if White recaptured: 2 bxc3 ♗a3+ 3 ♔b1 ♖d1+ 4 ♗c1 ♖xc1.

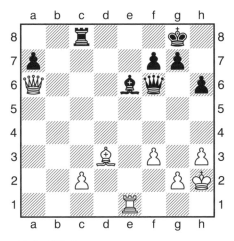

186) White moves

The h7-square – the black king's only potential escape route – *is controlled by the white bishop on d3*. White wins with 1 ♕xc8+ ♗xc8 2 ♖e8 mate.

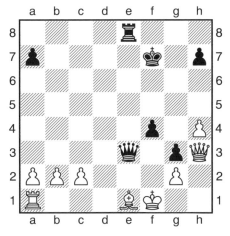

187) Black moves

After 1...♕e2+ 2 ♔g1 ♕xe1+ 3 ♖xe1 ♖xe1 White is mated on the back rank. The black pawn on g3 is controlling two crucial flight squares, h2 and f2.

Rook Deflections

When the guard leaves his post...

Although easy to misclassify, a *deflecting* sacrifice is subtly different from a decoy sacrifice. In a decoy sacrifice, an opponent's piece is decoyed *onto a specific square*. In a deflection, a piece is deflected *away from* a particular point. It does not really matter where the deflected piece ends up; the idea is simply that it ceases to perform its former defensive function.

Rooks are excellent pieces for making deflecting sacrifices on the eighth rank. Usually this involves deflecting other rooks! The result is typically a decisive gain of material, but checkmates are also possible.

Typical Patterns for the Rook Deflection

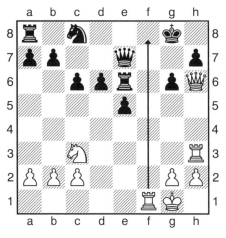

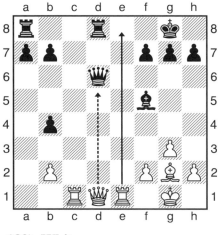

188) White moves

1 ♖f8+ *deflects the black queen from the defence of h7*. After the forced capture 1...♕xf8, White plays 2 ♕xh7 checkmate.

189) White moves

Here White wins the black queen with 1 ♖e8+ ♖xe8 2 ♕xd6. The sacrifice *deflected the black rook from its role of defending the queen on d6.*

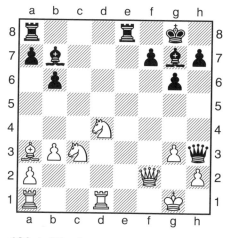

190a) Black moves

The stunning move 1...♖e1+! aims to deflect the white queen, currently guarding against ...♕g2 mate by Black. After 2 ♖xe1 comes 2...♗xd4 (190b).

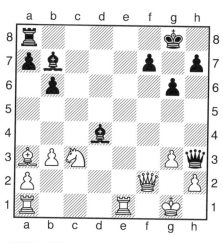

190b) White moves

The white rook has been deflected from d1, and cannot capture the bishop on d4. After 2 ♕xd4 (or White loses the queen) Black plays 2...♕g2 mate.

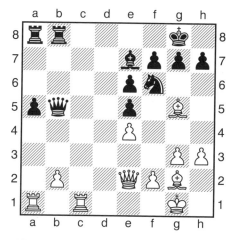

191) White moves

This is most common type of rook deflection. 1 ♖c8+ wins, as after 1...♗f8 White can win a rook with 2 ♕xb5 ♖xb5 3 ♖xa8.

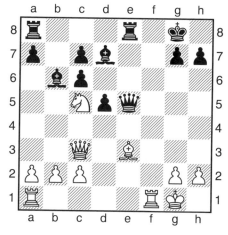

192) White moves

The pretty 1 ♖f8+! is both a decoy (after 1...♔xf8 2 ♘xd7+, forking king and queen) and a deflection (1...♖xf8 2 ♕xe5, winning the black queen).

DEADLY CHECKMATE 44   Two Rooks on the Seventh

Not so blind swine...

Two rooks on the seventh rank can be a truly mighty force – akin to a tornado on the chessboard. Stray pawns are whisked away as the two rooks go on the rampage, checking and terrorizing the opposing king.

As the rooks mutually support each other, they can create repeated mating threats, and their presence can virtually paralyse the defence. In spite of this, the two rooks are usually unable to force mate in the middlegame on their own. The assistance of one other attacking unit (piece or pawn) is generally needed to do the trick.

Sometimes two rooks on the seventh are only good enough for a draw by perpetual check, or repetition of position. This occurs when the opponent is material ahead or has his own serious threats. Two rooks which can only 'grunt out check', but not mate, were dubbed *Blind Swine* by the famous attacking player Dawid Janowsky.

Typical Patterns for Mate with Two Rooks on the Seventh

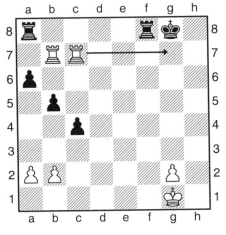

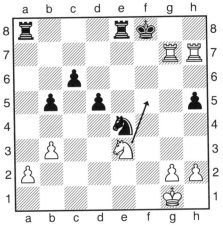

193) White moves

The black king has no flight square on f8, it being occupied by his own rook. White administers checkmate with 1 ♖g7+ ♔h8 2 ♖h7+ ♔g8 3 ♖bg7.

194) White moves

Here mate is not possible with the rooks alone – an extra piece must assist. 1 ♘f5 (protecting the rook on g7) sets up the unstoppable threat of 2 ♖h8.

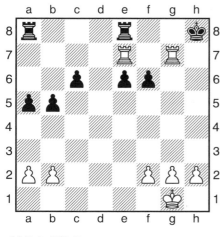

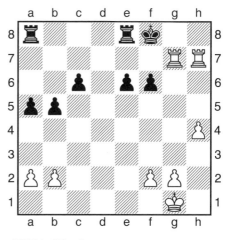

195a) White moves

The rooks dominate the seventh rank beautifully. But to win White must introduce an extra attacking unit: 1 ♖h7+ ♚g8 2 ♖eg7+ ♚f8 3 h4! *(195b)*.

195b) Black moves

The advance of the h-pawn decides! White plan is h5 and h6 (protecting the rook on g7), followed by ♖h8 mate. Black cannot set up a defence.

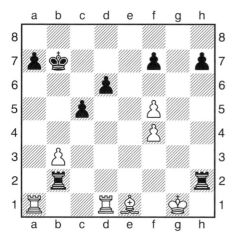

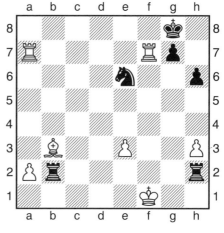

196) Black moves

A piece down, Black salvages the draw with *perpetual threats*: 1...♖bg2+ 2 ♚f1 ♖b2 (threatening 3...♖h1 mate) 3 ♚g1 ♖bg2+ 4 ♚f1, etc.

197) White moves

Both players have rooks on the seventh, but White is to move *and* his bishop assists: 1 ♖xg7+ ♚f8 2 ♖af7+ ♚e8 3 ♗a4+ ♚d8 4 ♖g8+ ♘f8 5 ♖gxf8 mate.

DEADLY CHECKMATE 45

Anderssen's Mate

Watch out for those 'horrible bishops'

The name is derived from the beautiful game Anderssen-Zukertort, Barmen 1869, where White sacrificed a queen and then a bishop to force checkmate. Anderssen's Mate involves *a sacrifice on h7* – to open the h-file and expose the black king – followed by *checkmate on the h8-square*. There are two circumstances where this type of combination is extremely likely to be possible:

1) When White has a pair of 'Horwitz bishops'[1] raking the b1-h7 and a1-h8 diagonals, and *Black is missing a defensive g-pawn on g7 or g6*.

2) When White has a pawn on the g7-square, directly in front of the black king.

Typical Pattern for Anderssen's Mate

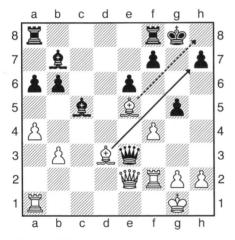

198a) White moves

As Black is missing a defensive pawn on g7 or g6 the white bishops control many kingside squares. White sacrifices with 1 ♗xh7+ ♔xh7 *(198b)*.

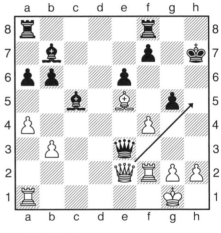

198b) White moves

The white queen exploits the newly opened h-file with 2 ♕h5+ ♔g8 3 ♕h8 checkmate.

---

1 'Horwitz bishops' (also known as Parallel or Raking Bishops) refers to a pair of bishops aggressively placed on adjacent diagonals.

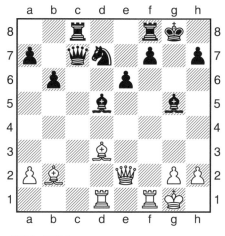

199) White moves

After 1 ♗xh7+ ♔xh7 2 ♕h5+ ♗h6 Black has avoided the mate on h8, but White wins with the continuation 3 ♖xf7+ ♖xf7 4 ♕xf7+ ♗g7 5 ♕xg7 mate.

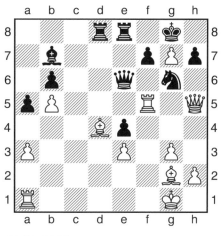

200) White moves

A white pawn lodged on g7 controls the h8-square – and can even promote to a queen: 1 ♕xh7+ ♔xh7 2 ♖h5+ ♔g8 3 ♖h8+ ♘xh8 4 gxh8♕ mate.

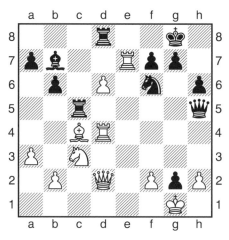

201a) Black moves

The g2-pawn is protected (by the bishop on b7) and a black rook can reach the h-file. There follows the queen sacrifice 1...♕xh2+ 2 ♔xh2 ♖h5+ *(201b)*.

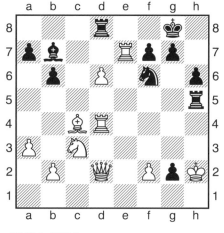

201b) White moves

3 ♔g1 fails to 3...♖h1 mate. However, advancing with 3 ♔g3 is equally disastrous, as Black will mate in two moves with 3...g1♕+ 4 ♔f4 ♕g5.

DEADLY CHECKMATE 46 — Pawn on the Seventh Rank

A new queen – in the middlegame!

A pawn that has reached the seventh rank makes all sorts of magical combinations possible. This is especially so when a pawn is on g7 or h7, and the opposing king is sitting directly in front of it, on the eighth rank.

Such a far-advanced pawn controls some valuable squares, which can greatly assist some mating attacks. Deadly Checkmate 45, Anderssen's Mate, showed some examples of this.

Even more deadly is also the possibility of a *decoy sacrifice* in order to force promotion of the pawn.

Typical Pattern with a Pawn on the Seventh Rank

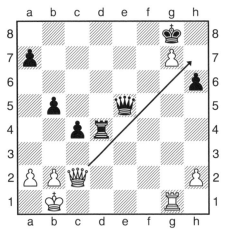

202a) White moves

Material is equal. Black would be fine – except for the dramatic queen sacrifice 1 ♕h7+! ♚xh7 *(202b)*, decoying the black king.

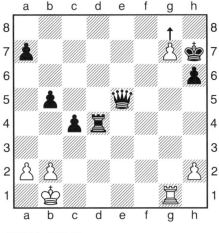

202b) White moves

White promotes his g-pawn with 2 g8♕. The pawn becomes a queen, and Black's king is checkmated.

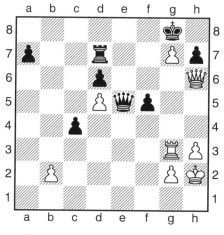

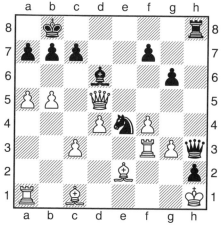

203) White moves

Although the white rook is pinned, the thematic combination is still possible: 1 ♕xh7+ ♔xh7 2 g8♕+ ♔h6 3 ♕g6 mate.

204) Black moves

The win is 1...♕g2+ 2 ♔xg2 h1♕ mate. Note how Black gave up a whole queen to force the h-pawn through to promotion, and thus deliver checkmate.

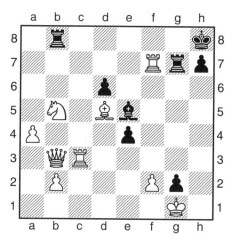

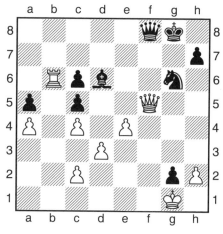

205) Black moves

The sacrifice 1...♗h2+ forces the white king to vacate the g1-square, allowing the black pawn on g2 to advance. 2 ♔xh2 g1♕+ 3 ♔h3 ♕h1 is mate.

206) Black moves

A magical example: 1...♗xh2+! 2 ♔xh2 ♕h6+ wins. Then 3 ♔g2 ♘h4+ forks king and queen, whilst 3 ♔g3 g1♕+ and 3 ♔g1 ♕h1+ are also decisive.

Legall's Mate

Legall's pseudo-sacrifice is even more common...

Legall's famous mate usually occurs in the opening stage of the game and involves White *breaking a pin*. It arises when Black has a bishop on g4, pinning a white knight on f3 against the white queen on d1. White will therefore lose his valuable queen if the knight moves, but in exceptional positions White can offer a sacrifice (usually by playing ♘e5). The idea is that if Black captures the queen, White's minor pieces will deliver checkmate in one or two moves.

Legall's Mate is only seen at beginner level, but a refined version (*Legall's Pseudo-Sacrifice*) can trap anyone. White does not have a forced checkmate after giving up his queen, but instead wins material with a powerful bishop check on b5.

Typical Pattern for Legall's Mate

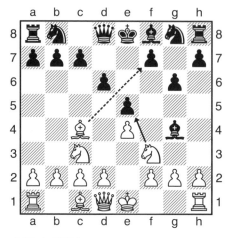

207a) White moves

After 1 ♘xe5 Black captures the white queen with 1...♗xd1 (as 1...dxe5 2 ♕xg4 would win a pawn for White). White continues 2 ♗xf7+ *(207b)*.

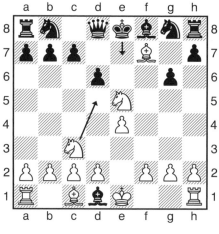

207b) Black moves

The black king's only move is 2...♔e7, and White replies 3 ♘d5 mate. White needs *three* attacking minor pieces to force mate in this version.

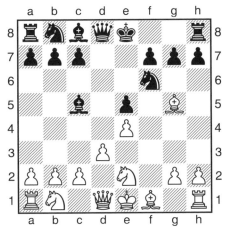

208) Black moves

In this case it is possible to mate with just two minor pieces, as the e2-square is blocked by White's own knight. Black plays 1...♘xe4 2 ♗xd8 ♗f2 mate.

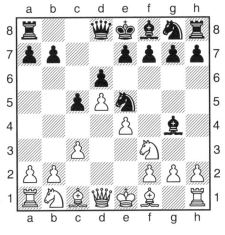

209) White moves

A typical example of *Legall's Pseudo-Sacrifice*. 1 ♘xe5 ♗xd1 2 ♗b5+ wins material, because Black must interpose with 2...♕d7, giving back the queen.

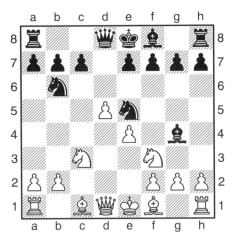

210a) White moves

The pin is broken with 1 ♘xe5. White sacrifices the queen, in spite of the fact that 1...♗xd1 2 ♗b5+ c6 *(210b)* enables Black to block the bishop check.

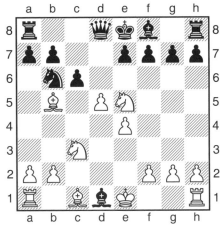

210b) White moves

After 3 dxc6 Black is helpless against the potential discovered checks (4 cxb7+ and 4 c7+), e.g. 3...a6 4 c7+ or 3...♕c7 4 cxb7+ ♔d8 5 ♘xf7 mate.

107

The Bishop Sacrifice on f7

Winning right in the opening

The f7-square is Black's most vulnerable point prior to castling. However, Black's *lack* of development is not the primary cause of 'accidents' on this square. *Awkward* piece placement is the main reason. A common mistake is for Black to start developing the queenside minor pieces before his kingside minor pieces. There are then two standard scenarios where White can play the crushing ♗xf7+ sacrifice.

1) The black knight moves to d7 prematurely

The manoeuvre ♗xf7+, followed by ♘g5+ and ♘e6 often wins immediately. *As the black bishop on c8 no longer controls the e6-square, White's knight can potentially use this square.*

2) The black bishop moves to g4 prematurely

Often this is a tactical blunder. After ♗xf7+ ♔xf7 White plays ♘g5+ (or sometimes ♘e5+) and the black bishop on g4 is under attack from White's queen on d1.

Typical Pattern for the ♗xf7+ Sacrifice

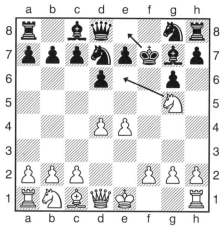

211a) White moves

The black knight has been developed to d7 prematurely, weakening control of the e6-square. White sacrifices with 1 ♗xf7+ ♔xf7 2 ♘g5+ *(211b)*.

211b) Black moves

The king, in check from White's knight, has no good square. If 2...♔f6, 3 ♕f3 mate; if 2...♔f8, 3 ♘e6+, and if 2...♔e8, then 3 ♘e6 traps the black queen.

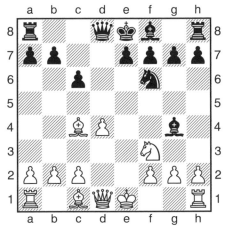

212) White moves

A pawn is won by using the black bishop on g4 as a target. After 1 ♗xf7+ ♚xf7 2 ♘e5+ Black's king must move. White regains the bishop with 3 ♘xg4.

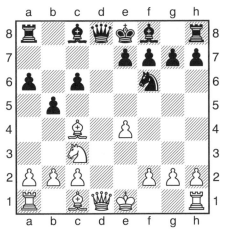

213) White moves

Where the d-file is opened very early, watch out for the typical deflecting sacrifice 1 ♗xf7+ ♚xf7 2 ♕xd8 winning the black queen.

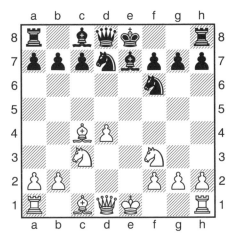

214a) White moves

Black is as well developed as White, but his pieces are *momentarily awkwardly placed*. White must pounce swiftly: 1 ♗xf7+ ♚xf7 2 ♘g5+ *(214b)*.

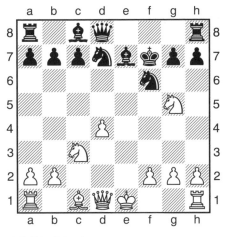

214b) Black moves

The retreat 1...♚g8 gets mated by 2 ♕b3+. However, after 1...♚g6 2 ♕d3+ ♚h5 3 ♕f5 Black's exposed king will soon perish as well.

109

Knight Sacrifices on f7 & e6

Making sure Dad will never get castled

There are similarities here with Deadly Checkmate 48. Early in the game, before castling, a king is vulnerable to piece sacrifices which eliminate its central pawn shelter. Once again, it is not *necessarily* a lack of development that allows the crushing piece sacrifice. Sometimes Black's pieces are just unfortunately placed.

1) Knight sacrifice on f7

There are several possible ideas behind this. The elimination of the f7-pawn removes a key defender of the e6-square. Alternatively White may wish to open the h5-e8 diagonal, or to lure the black king to f7 so another piece can follow up with check.

2) Knight Sacrifice on e6

Here the plan is either to exterminate the central pawns, or to exploit the h5-e8 diagonal (which becomes open when Black captures the knight with ...fxe6).

Typical Pattern for the Knight Sacrifice on f7

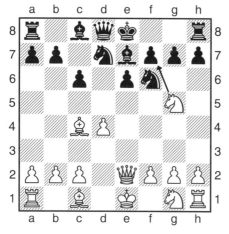

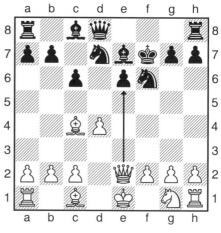

215a) White moves

In principle Black has a solid position, but he is one move away from castling to safety. White seizes his chance with the knight sacrifice 1 ♘xf7 ♚xf7 *(215b)*.

215b) White moves

After 2 ♕xe6+ Black's defensive pawns have vanished. On 2...♚e8 or 2...♚f8 White has 3 ♕f7 mate, and if 2...♚g6, 3 ♗d3+ ♚h5 4 ♕h3 is mate.

110

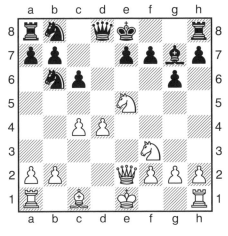

216) White moves

Eliminating the f7-pawn *weakens Black's control of the e6-square*. White plays 1 ♘xf7 ♔xf7 2 ♘g5+ ♔e8 3 ♘e6 forking queen and bishop.

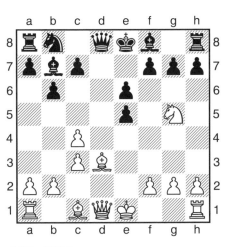

217) White moves

1 ♘xf7 ♔xf7 2 ♗g6+ wins White a queen for two pieces following 2...hxg6 (after 2...♔e7 White has 3 ♗g5 mate) 3 ♕xd8. A well-hidden combination.

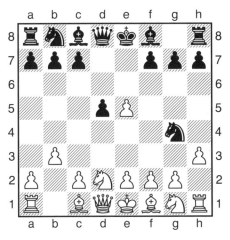

218) Black moves

This age-old trap shows the knight sacrifice used to prise open a vulnerable diagonal. 1...♘e3 2 fxe3 (or the queen is lost) 2...♕h4+ 3 g3 ♕xg3 mate.

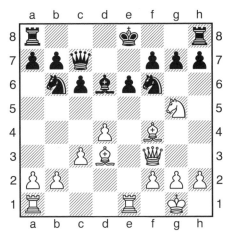

219) White moves

Black (who is one move from castling to safety) has his pawn-cover eliminated with the routine 1 ♘xe6 fxe6 2 ♖xe6+ followed by capturing the bishop on d6.

111

The Fischer Trap

Two sacrifices for the price of one

The great German player Siegbert Tarrasch (1862-1934) once fell for this checkmate. In 1958 America's legendary Bobby Fischer created his own famous version against Sammy Reshevsky.

The prerequisites for this nifty ruse are pretty basic. White needs a bishop attacking the black f7-pawn, and also a white knight that could move to the e6-square with great effect if the black f7-pawn were absent.

Under these conditions White can consider the possibility of sacrificing with ♗xf7+, intending the follow-up with ♘e6 next move. A clever feature, which fools many victims, arises when Black can capture the bishop with his king. This appears to maintain control of the e6-square. In fact White plays the powerful ♘e6 move anyway, offering the knight as an additional sacrifice. The black king is lured out into the centre, where checkmate virtually always follows.

Typical Pattern for the Fischer Trap

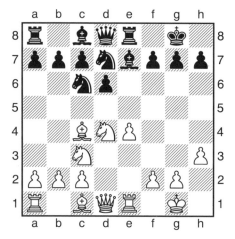

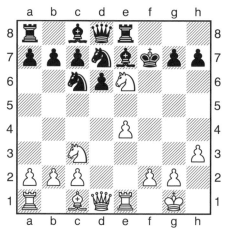

220a) White moves

The bishop is sacrificed with 1 ♗xf7+, forcing 1...♔xf7. Then comes the startling follow-up, 2 ♘e6 *(220b)*, attacking the black queen.

220b) Black moves

To avoid losing his queen, Black captures with 2...♔xe6. Now that the king is exposed in the centre. White continues 3 ♕d5+ ♔f6 4 ♕f5 checkmate.

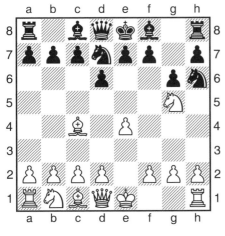

221) White moves

Here Black does not have the option of capturing on f7 with his king. White wins easily with 1 ♗xf7+ ♘xf7 2 ♘e6 trapping the black queen.

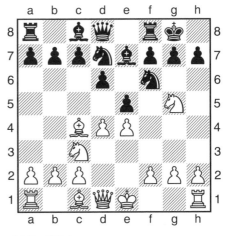

222) White moves

1 ♗xf7+ ♖xf7 2 ♘e6 ♕e8 3 ♘xc7 forks the black queen and rook. But a complication to consider is that after 3...♕d8 4 ♘xa8 the knight may be trapped.

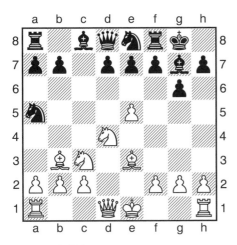

223a) White moves

The Fischer-Reshevsky game. Black's solid position was shattered with 1 ♗xf7+ ♔xf7 (1...♖xf7 2 ♘e6! dxe6 3 ♕xd8 wins the queen) 2 ♘e6 (223b).

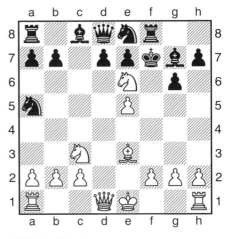

223b) Black moves

To save his queen Black plays 2...♔xe6 (if 2...dxe6, 3 ♕xd8). But after 3 ♕d5+ ♔f5 the black king perishes, e.g. 4 g4+ ♔xg4 5 ♖g1+ ♔h5 6 ♕d1+.

Test Positions

In each of these positions your task is to find the winning combination that either *forces checkmate* or *wins material*. All 36 positions are from real tournament games. If you can't find the idea immediately, *persevere with the challenge for at least 10 minutes per position*. If you need a hint after that, look up the *Deadly Checkmate(s)* listed next to each position to see the main motif you should be looking for.

Solutions are given on page 121.

Target Scores

If you tackle the tests without using the hints, the number of combinations correctly found corresponds to your ability roughly as follows:

All 36	**Master standard**
30-35	**Tournament strength player**
25-29	**Excellent Pattern Recognition**
20-24	**Good Pattern Recognition**
15-19	**Promising – join a chess club!**
10-14	**Average**
5-9	**More practice needed**
0-4	**Does Dad play backgammon?**

ANASTASIA'S MATE

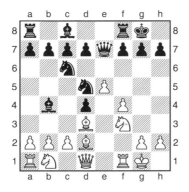

224) White moves.
Hint: see Checkmate 32.

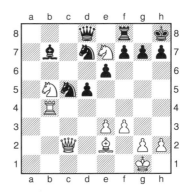

225) White moves.
Hint: see Checkmate 1.

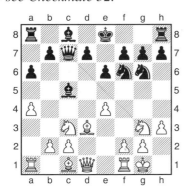

226) Black moves.
Hint: see Checkmate 28.

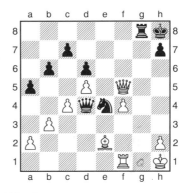

227) Black moves.
Hint: see Checkmate 5.

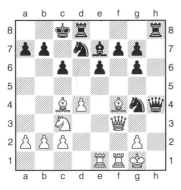

228) White moves.
Hint: see Checkmate 14.

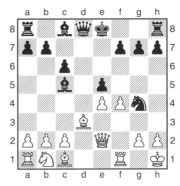

229) Black moves.
Hint: see Checkmate 2.

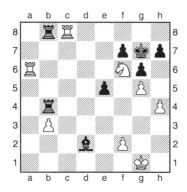

230) White moves.
Hint: see Checkmate 3.

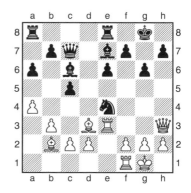

231) White moves.
Hint: see Checkmate 37.

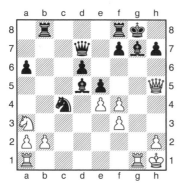

232) White moves.
Hint: see Checkmate 21.

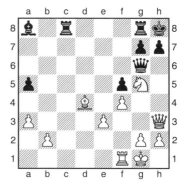

233) White moves.
Hint: see Checkmate 4.

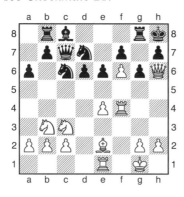

234) White moves.
Hint: see Checkmate 39.

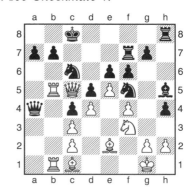

235) White moves.
Hint: see Checkmate 15.

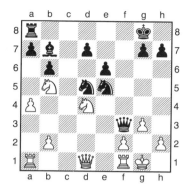

236) Black moves.
Hint: see Checkmate 38.

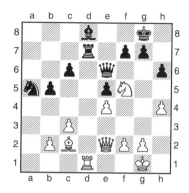

237) White moves.
Hint: see Checkmate 22.

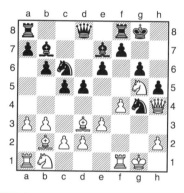

238) White moves.
Hint: see Checkmate 13.

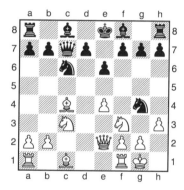

239) Black moves.
Hint: see Checkmate 31.

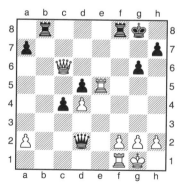

240) Black moves.
Hint: see Checkmate 41.

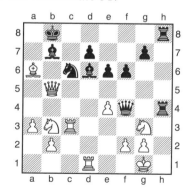

241) Black moves.
Hint: see Checkmate 7.

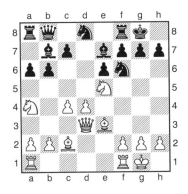

242) White moves.

Hint: see Checkmate 30.

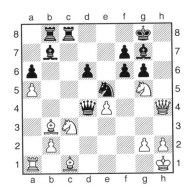

243) White moves.

Hint: see Checkmate 50.

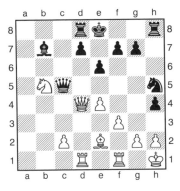

244) Black moves.

Hint: see Checkmates 9 & 6.

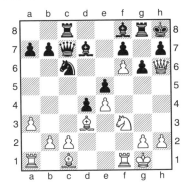

245) White moves.

Hint: see Checkmate 5.

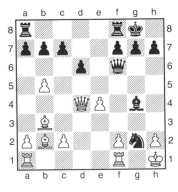

246) Black moves.

Hint: see Checkmate 38.

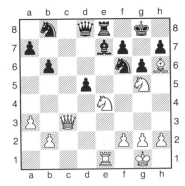

247) White moves.

Hint: see Checkmate 42.

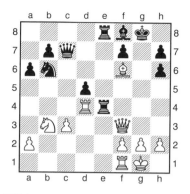

248) White moves.

Hint: see Checkmates 37 & 18.

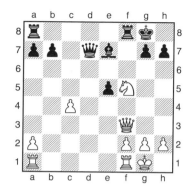

249) White moves.

Hint: see Checkmate 23.

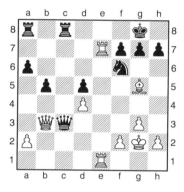

250) White moves.

Hint: see Checkmate 43.

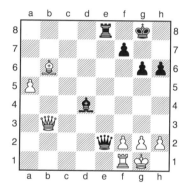

251) Black moves.

Hint: see Checkmate 41.

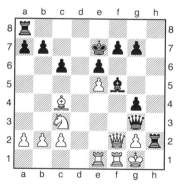

252) Black moves.

Hint: see Checkmate 6.

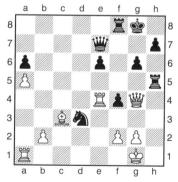

253) Black moves.

Hint: see Checkmate 12.

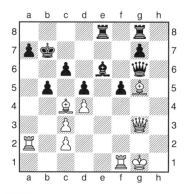

254) White moves.

Hint: see Checkmate 24.

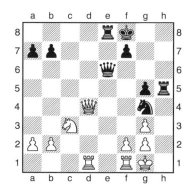

255) Black moves.

Hint: see Checkmate 6.

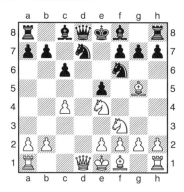

256) Black moves.

Hint: see Checkmate 47.

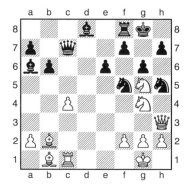

257) White moves.

Hint: see Checkmates 38 & 13.

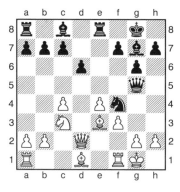

258) Black moves.

Hint: see Checkmate 22.

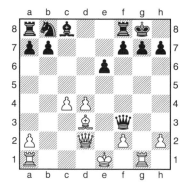

259) White moves.

Hint: see Checkmates 21 & 42.

Solutions to Test Positions

224. The classic *Greek Gift* sacrifice decides: 1 ♗xh7+ ♔xh7 2 ♘g5+ ♔g8 (if 2...♔g6, 3 f5+ wins) 3 ♕h5 and Black has no defence to ♕h7+ next move.

225. White uses the theme from *Anastasia's Mate*: 1 ♕xh7+ ♔xh7 2 ♖h4 checkmate.

226. Black wins a piece with 1...♕xg3 in a simple version of *Korchnoi's Manoeuvre*.

227. 1...♕g1+ 2 ♖xg1 ♘f2 is a neat *Semi-Smothered Mate*.

228. After a queen sacrifice the white bishops deliver *Boden's Mate* with 1 ♕xc6+ bxc6 2 ♗a6 mate.

229. 1...♘xh2 exploits the *Missing Defensive f-pawn*.

230. After 1 ♖a8 ♖xa8 (1...♖xc8 2 ♖xc8 makes no difference) 2 ♖xa8 Black cannot prevent the *Arabian Mate* with 3 ♖g8 next move.

231. *Weak Dark Squares* is the motif here. White's bishop raking the long diagonal assists the white rook in the mate with 1 ♕xh7+ ♔xh7 2 ♖h3+ ♔g8 3 ♖h8.

232. In this *Rook Sacrifice on g7* the white queen zigzags in before the second white rook delivers the mate: 1 ♖xg7+ ♔xg7 2 ♕g5+ ♔h8 3 ♕f6+ ♔g8 4 ♖g1+ ♕g4 5 ♖xg4.

233. 1 ♕xh7+ ♕xh7 2 ♘f7 is a *Smothered Mate* your Dad will hate.

234. White wins with a straightforward version of *Lolli's Mate*: 1 ♕xh7+ ♔xh7 2 ♖h4 checkmate.

235. 1 ♕xc6+ bxc6 2 ♖b8+ ♔d7 (or 2...♔c7) 3 ♖1b7 checkmate – the theme from *Other Queenside Mates*.

236. 1...♕g2+! 2 ♔xg2 ♘f4++ forces *Blackburne's Other Mate* after 3 ♔g1 ♘h3.

237. After a preliminary exchange of rooks the superb *Knight on f5* comes into its own. 1 ♖xd7 ♕xd7 2 ♕g4 and White threatens both mate on g7, and to win Black's queen with ♘xh6+.

238. The swashbuckling 1 ♕xh5 sets up *Blackburne's Mate* after 1...gxh5 2 ♗h7.

239. *Removing the f6 Defender* is the theme here (in fact it becomes the f3 defender with Black to move). 1...♘d4 wins after 2 ♕d1 (2 ♘xd4 ♕h2 mate) 2...♘xf3+ 3 ♕xf3 ♕h2 checkmate.

240. A *Refined Back-Rank Mate* does the trick: 1...♕xf2+ 2 ♖xf2 ♖b1+ 3 ♖f1 ♖(either)xf1 mate.

241. The theme is the *Double Rook Sacrifice on h8* (or h1 for Black). Here Black wins with 1...♖h1+ 2 ♘xh1 ♖xh1+ 3 ♔xh1 ♕h2 checkmate.

242. Profiting from the *Queen and Bishop Line-up*, White wins with 1 ♘d7, exploiting latent checkmate threats against h7. If 1...♘xd7, 2 ♕xh7 is mate, and if 1...♕c8, 2 ♘xf6+ ♗xf6 3 ♕xh7 mate.

243. An original version of the *Fischer Trap*. White wins the black queen with 1 ♗xf7+ ♘xf7 2 ♕h7+ ♔f8 3 ♘e6+ and next 4 ♘xd4.

244. *Taimanov's Knight Check* is first used to open the h-file followed by a *Single Rook Sacrifice* on the h1-square: 1...♘g3+ 2 hxg3 hxg3+ 3 ♔g1 ♖h1+ 4 ♔xh1 ♕h5+ 5 ♔g1 ♕h2 checkmate.

245. Another *Semi-Smothered Mate*: 1 ♘g5 ♗xh6 2 ♘xf7 checkmate.

246. 1...♗f3 2 ♕xf6 ♘f4+ 3 ♔g1 ♘h3 (or 3...♘e2) checkmate is *Blackburne's Other Mate*.

247. The *Back-Rank Mate* only works here if White gets the move-order right: 1 ♕xf6 (not 1 ♘xf6+ ♗xf6 2 ♖xe8+ ♕xe8 3 ♕xf6 and *Black* wins with the back-rank mate 3...♕e1) 1...♗xf6 2 ♘xf6+ and wins, as on 2...♕xf6, 3 ♖xe8 is checkmate.

248. 1 ♕g4+ ♖xg4 2 ♖xg4+ ♗g7 3 ♖xg7+ ♔f8 (3...♔h8 4 ♖g6 mate) 4 ♖xh7 with the unstoppable ♖h8 mate to follow is a mixture of *Weak Dark Squares* and *Morphy's Mate*.

249. The *Knight on f5* strikes again: 1 ♕d5+ ♕xd5 2 ♘xe7+ and White is a piece up after 3 ♘xd5 next move.

250. A *Rook Deflection* wins the black queen: 1 ♖e8+ ♘xe8 2 ♖xe8+ ♖xe8 3 ♕xc3.

251. 1...♕xf2+ 2 ♖xf2 ♖e1 checkmate: the most common version of the *Refined Back-Rank Mate*.

252. If Black's rook were on h8, not h2, mate with ...♕h2 would be possible. Black achieves this with a *Single Rook Sacrifice on the h-file*: 1...♖h1+ 2 ♔xh1 ♖h8+ 3 ♔g1 ♕h2 checkmate.

253. 1...♖h1+ 2 ♔xh1 ♘xf2+ forks the white king and queen – the old *♖h8+ & ♘xf7+ Trick* from Black's point of view.

254. The *Rook Decoy on h7* motif as played on the *queenside*: 1 ♖xa7+ ♔xa7 2 ♕c7+ ♔a8 (or 2...♔a6) 3 ♖a1 checkmate.

255. 1...♖h1+ 2 ♔xh1 ♕h6+ 3 ♔g1 ♕h2 checkmate is the *Single Rook Sacrifice* theme again. Note 1...♕h6 would fail to 2 ♕d6+, swapping queens.

256. Black breaks the pin with a variation on *Legall's Mate*: 1...♘xe4 2 ♗xd8 ♗b4+ 3 ♘d2 ♗xd2+ 4 ♕xd2 ♘xd2 winning a piece.

257. 1 ♕xh5 (not 1 ♗xf5 ♗xg5) wins with a lovely mixture of *Blackburne's Mate* and *Blackburne's Other Mate*: 1...gxh5 2 ♘h6+ ♘xh6 3 ♗xh7 mate.

258. 1...♗d4 is a clever exploitation of the *Knight on f5* theme (or, of course, a knight on f4 if Black is the attacker). 2 ♕xd4 allows 2...♕g2 mate, while 2 ♗xd4 loses the queen to 2...♘h3+ 3 ♔h1 ♕xd2. That leaves 2 ♖e1 ♗xe3+ 3 ♖xe3 ♘xg2 4 ♕xg2 ♕xe3+ winning.

259. Here the *Rook Sacrifice on g7* wins with minimal back-up because after 1 ♖xg7+ ♔xg7 2 ♕g5+ ♔h8 3 ♕h6 White threatens *Mate on the Back Rank* (with ♕xf8) as well as ♕xh7 mate.

Glossary of Terms

Breaking the Pin – If, as part of a combination, a pinned piece nevertheless moves, this is called *Breaking the Pin*.

Decoy – A sacrifice made to lure an enemy piece *onto* a particular square. Many Decoy sacrifices could also be called Deflections (see below), and the terms are often interchangeable.

Deflection – A deflecting sacrifice lures an enemy piece *away* from a particular square.

Double Attack – *Most chess combinations are based on this motif.* Two threats are made simultaneously, with the aim being that the defender can only deal with one.

Double Check – When the king is placed in check from two pieces simultaneously.

Exchange Sacrifice – A sacrifice of a rook (worth 5 points) for either a knight or a bishop (worth 3 points each).

Exchange, the – When one side is a rook for either knight or bishop ahead, they are said to be 'the exchange' ahead. 'Winning the exchange' is a common chess term, meaning one side has won a rook for either a bishop or a knight.

Fianchettoed Bishop – A bishop that is developed on the long diagonal after moving the g-pawn or b-pawn one square forward. For example, if White has pawns on h2, g3 and f2, a bishop on g2 is said to be *fianchettoed*.

Flight Square – An escape square for the king.

Fork – Where two pieces (or more) are simultaneously attacked by one opposing piece, in such a way that material loss is forced.

Horwitz Bishops – Two bishops lined up on adjacent diagonals, pointing directly at the enemy king. Also known as *Parallel* or *Raking* bishops.

Long Diagonal – The diagonals a1-h8 and h1-a8 are called the long diagonals.

Major Pieces – This refers to the queens and rooks (sometimes also called the Heavy Pieces).

Mating-Net – A king caught in a formation where forced mate is inevitable, even though it may take a few moves.

Minor Pieces – Bishops and knights are known as the *minor pieces*.

Open File – A file containing *no pawns of either colour*. Usually rooks are well-placed on such files, as they can move freely along them.

Overloaded Piece – Where a piece has more than one important defensive duty, and *cannot perform them all*, it is said to be overloaded.

Parallel Bishops – see Horwitz bishops.

Perpetual Check – Where one side can give check indefinitely, thus eventually leading to a draw.

Pin – If a piece cannot move without exposing a more valuable piece behind it to attack, then it is said to be *pinned*.

Raking Bishops – see Horwitz Bishops.

Semi-open File – A file containing a pawn or pawns of only one colour. Semi-open files are very useful for attacking the king with the *major pieces* – the rooks and the queens.

Skewer – A material-winning manoeuvre, performed by bishops, rooks or queens. A enemy piece is attacked and forced to move out of the way, so that a piece of lesser value behind it can be won.

Spite Check – A check of no practical value made in a lost position, usually merely to prolong a lost game or put off checkmate for another move.

Swindle – A devious trick that saves or wins a clearly lost game, or wins a patently drawn game.

Tempo – The unit of time taken by one move. A move made 'with tempo' is a move that performs a useful purpose while gaining time by means of a strong secondary threat (such as a check or an attack on a piece).

Vacating Sacrifice – A sacrifice made to *vacate the square a piece stands on*, so that it can be used by another piece of the same colour.

X-Ray Attack – An attack along a file or diagonal *where the effect continues through and beyond an intervening enemy piece* (see diagram 152 for an example).

THE SEE-SAW

And Finally ...

What to do if Your Dad is Garry Kasparov

It has to be admitted that if your Dad is one of the greatest chess players of all time, you have a bit of a problem! However, do not give up hope. First of all, let's establish that it is perfectly possible to beat Kasparov with the themes from this book, as the following examples show:

Karpov – Kasparov
World Ch. (game 3), Moscow 1984/5

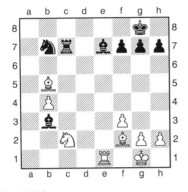

260) White moves

Karpov won with 1 ♗b6, as on 1...♖xc2 2 ♖xe7 Kasparov will lose his knight or be *Back-Rank Mated.* For example 2...♘d6 3 ♗c5 ♘xb5 4 ♖e8 checkmate. Easy!

Short – Kasparov
Brussels 1986

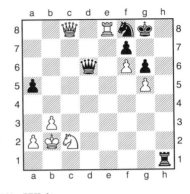

261) White moves

Here the *Weak Dark Squares* (caused by the white pawn lodged on f6) assist in Kasparov's demise. After 1 ♖d8 ♕e5+ 2 ♔a3 Black can no longer defend against the threat of 3 ♖xf8+.

Topalov – Kasparov
Moscow Olympiad 1994

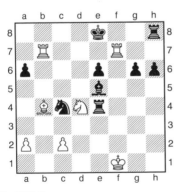

262) White moves

The mighty power of the *Two rooks on the Seventh Rank* caused Kasparov's downfall here. White wins with 1 ♖fe7+ ♔d8 2 ♘c6+ as on 2...♔c8 there follows 3 ♘a7+ ♔d8 4 ♖bd7 checkmate.

Svidler – Kasparov
Tilburg 1997

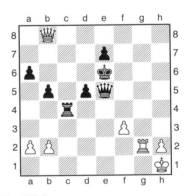

263) White moves

Here Peter Svidler wrapped up the game by threatening to win Kasparov's queen with a *Rook Decoy Sacrifice.* 1 ♖g6+ ♔f5 2 ♖g5+! ♔xg5 3 ♕xe5+ uses the same motif as Deadly Checkmate 24.

As these Kasparov losses show, even champions are helpless against the basic attacking themes. The difficulty – of course – is achieving the advantageous position in the first place. If you want to become a *really* strong player – a potential chess master – you will need to work on all aspects of your game.

We conclude with some tips to guide you once you have mastered the important motifs in this book. They work even if your Dad isn't Garry Kasparov...

For Further Improvement

1) Play lots of games

Fast games, slow games, friendly or serious – play all the time, preferably against opponents a little stronger than yourself. When possible have a *post-mortem* afterwards, where you discuss the game with your opponent and compare thoughts. A top PC chess playing program (like Fritz or Chess Genius) will also provide good practice.

2) Read lots of chess books

There is a wonderful range of chess literature. Study the openings, middlegames and endings. You can do all three at once by playing through a good games collection of a great player. Subscribe to a regular chess magazine, and play over lots of grandmaster games quite quickly to develop a 'feel' for the way strong players develop their pieces and prepare attacks.

3) Develop an Opening Repertoire

How you open a game is very important, as a good opening will help you gain an attacking position. Don't be scared of 'theory', but instead use it to your advantage! It is great fun to see systems you have studied from books at home appear on the board.

When you join a chess club, and start playing tournaments, always keep a record of your games, and look up the openings afterwards.

4) Concentrate hard

Top chess masters develop great powers of concentration, as *they know that the most amazing nuances can be hidden in almost any position.* You must work very, very hard, calculating and analysing variations during a game. Don't be superficial in your thinking – and treat *all* opponents with respect.

5) Attack with confidence

If you get an advantage in position, be bold! Even if Kasparov is your Dad, *he can't save a lost position if you attack perfectly.* If you do get a chance, launch a direct assault on the enemy king.

*Other chess books
produced by ...*

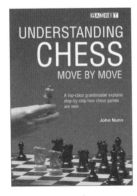
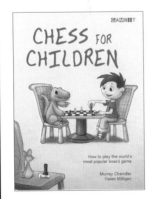